Singapore Math Practice

LEVEL 4B

Appropriate for Students in GRADE 5

Frank Schaffer
An imprint of Carson-Dellosa Publishing LLC
Greensboro, North Carolina

Copyright © 2009 Singapore Asian Publications (S) Pte. Ltd.

Frank Schaffer
An imprint of Carson-Dellosa Publishing LLC
PO Box 35665
Greensboro, NC 27425 USA

The purchase of this material entitles the buyer to reproduce worksheets and activities for classroom use only—not for commercial resale. Reproduction of these materials for an entire school or district is prohibited. No part of this book may be reproduced (except as noted above), stored in a retrieval system, or transmitted in any form or by any means (mechanically, electronically, recording, etc.) without the prior written consent of Carson-Dellosa Publishing LLC. Frank Schaffer is an imprint of Carson-Dellosa Publishing LLC.

Printed in the USA • All rights reserved.
3 4 5 6 GLO 13 12 11 10

ISBN 978-0-7682-4004-7
260107784

INTRODUCTION TO SINGAPORE MATH

Welcome to Singapore Math! The math curriculum in Singapore has been recognized worldwide for its excellence in producing students highly skilled in mathematics. Students in Singapore have ranked at the top in the world in mathematics on the *Trends in International Mathematics and Science Study* (TIMSS) in 1993, 1995, 2003, and 2008. Because of this, Singapore Math has gained in interest and popularity in the United States.

Singapore Math curriculum aims to help students develop the necessary math concepts and process skills for everyday life and to provide students with the ability to formulate, apply, and solve problems. Mathematics in the Singapore Primary (Elementary) Curriculum cover fewer topics but in greater depth. Key math concepts are introduced and built-on to reinforce various mathematical ideas and thinking. Students in Singapore are typically one grade level ahead of students in the United States.

The following pages provide examples of the various math problem types and skill sets taught in Singapore.

At an elementary level, some simple mathematical skills can help students understand mathematical principles. These skills are the counting-on, counting-back, and crossing-out methods. Note that these methods are most useful when the numbers are small.

1. **The Counting-On Method**

   Used for addition of two numbers. Count on in 1s with the help of a picture or number line.

   $7 + 4 = 11$

   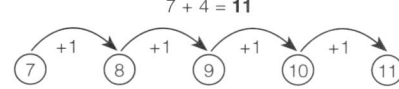

2. **The Counting-Back Method**

   Used for subtraction of two numbers. Count back in 1s with the help of a picture or number line.

   $16 - 3 = 13$

   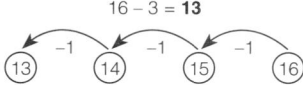

3. **The Crossing-Out Method**

   Used for subtraction of two numbers. Cross out the number of items to be taken away. Count the remaining ones to find the answer.

   $20 - 12 = 8$

A **number bond** shows the relationship in a simple addition or subtraction problem. The number bond is based on the concept "part-part-whole." This concept is useful in teaching simple addition and subtraction to young children.

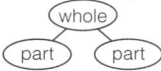

To find a whole, students must add the two parts.
To find a part, students must subtract the other part from the whole.

The different types of number bonds are illustrated below.

1. **Number Bond (single digits)**

   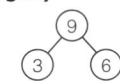

   3 (part) + 6 (part) = **9** (whole)
   9 (whole) − 3 (part) = **6** (part)
   9 (whole) − 6 (part) = **3** (part)

2. **Addition Number Bond (single digits)**

   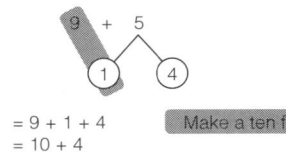

   = 9 + 1 + 4   Make a ten first.
   = 10 + 4
   = **14**

3. **Addition Number Bond (double and single digits)**

   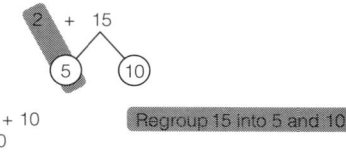

   = 2 + 5 + 10   Regroup 15 into 5 and 10.
   = 7 + 10
   = **17**

4. **Subtraction Number Bond (double and single digits)**

   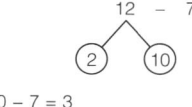

   $10 - 7 = 3$
   $3 + 2 = $ **5**

5. **Subtraction Number Bond (double digits)**

   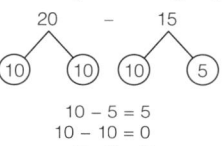

   $10 - 5 = 5$
   $10 - 10 = 0$
   $5 + 0 = $ **5**

Students should understand that multiplication is repeated addition and that division is the grouping of all items into equal sets.

1. **Repeated Addition (Multiplication)**

   Mackenzie eats 2 rolls a day. How many rolls does she eat in 5 days?

   $2 + 2 + 2 + 2 + 2 = 10$
   $5 \times 2 = 10$

   She eats **10** rolls in 5 days.

2. **The Grouping Method (Division)**

   Mrs. Lee makes 14 sandwiches. She gives all the sandwiches equally to 7 friends. How many sandwiches does each friend receive?

   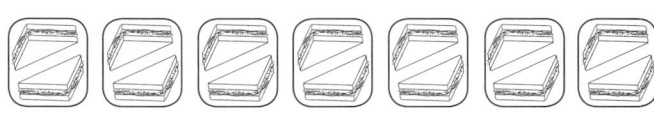

   $14 \div 7 = 2$

   Each friend receives **2** sandwiches.

One of the basic but essential math skills students should acquire is to perform the 4 operations of whole numbers and fractions. Each of these methods is illustrated below.

1. **The Adding-Without-Regrouping Method**

   ```
     H T O
     3 2 1        O: Ones
   + 5 6 8        T: Tens
   -------        H: Hundreds
     8 8 9
   ```

   Since no regrouping is required, add the digits in each place value accordingly.

2. **The Adding-by-Regrouping Method**

   ```
     H T O
    ¹4 9 2        O: Ones
   + 1 5 3        T: Tens
   -------        H: Hundreds
     6 4 5
   ```

   In this example, regroup 14 tens into 1 hundred 4 tens.

Singapore Math Practice Level 4B

3. **The Adding-by-Regrouping-Twice Method**

    ```
      H  T  O
     ¹2 ⁸6
    + 3  6  5
    ─────────
      6  5  1
    ```
    O: Ones
    T: Tens
    H: Hundreds

    Regroup twice in this example.
    First, regroup 11 ones into 1 ten 1 one.
    Second, regroup 15 tens into 1 hundred 5 tens.

4. **The Subtracting-Without-Regrouping Method**

    ```
      H  T  O
      7  3  9
    - 3  2  5
    ─────────
      4  1  4
    ```
    O: Ones
    T: Tens
    H: Hundreds

    Since no regrouping is required, subtract the digits in each place value accordingly.

5. **The Subtracting-by-Regrouping Method**

    ```
       H   T   O
       5  ⁷8 ¹¹1
    -  2   4   7
    ─────────────
       3   3   4
    ```
    O: Ones
    T: Tens
    H: Hundreds

    In this example, students cannot subtract 7 ones from 1 one. So, regroup the tens and ones. Regroup 8 tens 1 one into 7 tens 11 ones.

6. **The Subtracting-by-Regrouping-Twice Method**

    ```
       H   T   O
      ⁷8  ⁹0 ¹⁰0
    -  5   9   3
    ─────────────
       2   0   7
    ```
    O: Ones
    T: Tens
    H: Hundreds

    In this example, students cannot subtract 3 ones from 0 ones and 9 tens from 0 tens. So, regroup the hundreds, tens, and ones. Regroup 8 hundreds into 7 hundreds 9 tens 10 ones.

7. **The Multiplying-Without-Regrouping Method**

    ```
       T  O
       2  4
    ×     2
    ───────
       4  8
    ```
    O: Ones
    T: Tens

    Since no regrouping is required, multiply the digit in each place value by the multiplier accordingly.

8. **The Multiplying-With-Regrouping Method**

    ```
       H   T   O
          ¹3  ²4  9
    ×              3
    ──────────────
       1,  0   4   7
    ```
    O: Ones
    T: Tens
    H: Hundreds

    In this example, regroup 27 ones into 2 tens 7 ones, and 14 tens into 1 hundred 4 tens.

9. **The Dividing-Without-Regrouping Method**

    ```
           2 4 1
         ┌──────
       2 │ 4 8 2
          -4
          ──
           8
          -8
          ──
             2
            -2
            ──
             0
    ```

    Since no regrouping is required, divide the digit in each place value by the divisor accordingly.

10. **The Dividing-With-Regrouping Method**

    ```
            1 6 6
          ┌──────
        5 │ 8 3 0
           -5
           ──
            3 3
           -3 0
           ────
              3 0
             -3 0
             ────
                0
    ```

    In this example, regroup 3 hundreds into 30 tens and add 3 tens to make 33 tens. Regroup 3 tens into 30 ones.

11. **The Addition-of-Fractions Method**

    $$\frac{1 \times 2}{6 \times 2} + \frac{1 \times 3}{4 \times 3} = \frac{2}{12} + \frac{3}{12} = \frac{5}{12}$$

    Always remember to make the denominators common before adding the fractions.

12. **The Subtraction-of-Fractions Method**

    $$\frac{1 \times 5}{2 \times 5} - \frac{1 \times 2}{5 \times 2} = \frac{5}{10} - \frac{2}{10} = \frac{3}{10}$$

    Always remembers to make the denominators common before subtracting the fractions.

13. **The Multiplication-of-Fractions Method**

    $$\frac{\cancel{3}^1}{5} \times \frac{1}{\cancel{9}_3} = \frac{1}{15}$$

    When the numerator and the denominator have a common multiple, reduce them to their lowest fractions.

14. **The Division-of-Fractions Method**

    $$\frac{7}{9} \div \frac{1}{6} = \frac{7}{\cancel{9}_3} \times \frac{\cancel{6}^2}{1} = \frac{14}{3} = 4\frac{2}{3}$$

    When dividing fractions, first change the division sign (÷) to the multiplication sign (×). Then, switch the numerator and denominator of the fraction on the right hand side. Multiply the fractions in the usual way.

Model drawing is an effective strategy used to solve math word problems. It is a visual representation of the information in word problems using bar units. By drawing the models, students will know of the variables given in the problem, the variables to find, and even the methods used to solve the problem.

Drawing models is also a versatile strategy. It can be applied to simple word problems involving addition, subtraction, multiplication, and division. It can also be applied to word problems related to fractions, decimals, percentage, and ratio.

The use of models also trains students to think in an algebraic manner, which uses symbols for representation.

The different types of bar models used to solve word problems are illustrated below.

1. **The model that involves addition**

    Melissa has 50 blue beads and 20 red beads. How many beads does she have altogether?

    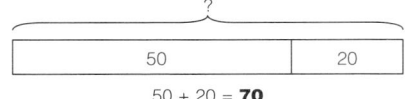

    50 + 20 = **70**

2. **The model that involves subtraction**

    Ben and Andy have 90 toy cars. Andy has 60 toy cars. How many toy cars does Ben have?

    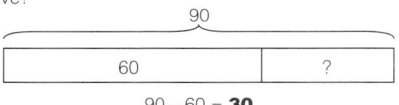

    90 − 60 = **30**

3. **The model that involves comparison**

    Mr. Simons has 150 magazines and 110 books in his study. How many more magazines than books does he have?

    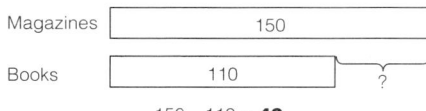

    150 − 110 = **40**

4. **The model that involves two items with a difference**

    A pair of shoes costs $109. A leather bag costs $241 more than the pair of shoes. How much is the leather bag?

    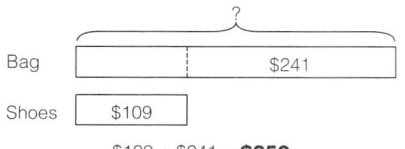

    $109 + $241 = **$350**

Singapore Math Practice Level 4B

5. The model that involves multiples

Mrs. Drew buys 12 apples. She buys 3 times as many oranges as apples. She also buys 3 times as many cherries as oranges. How many pieces of fruit does she buy altogether?

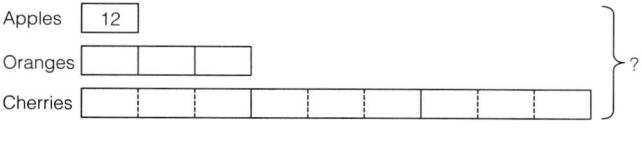

13 × 12 = **156**

6. The model that involves multiples and difference

There are 15 students in Class A. There are 5 more students in Class B than in Class A. There are 3 times as many students in Class C than in Class A. How many students are there altogether in the three classes?

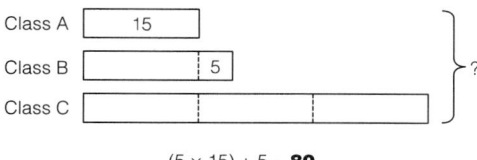

(5 × 15) + 5 = **80**

7. The model that involves creating a whole

Ellen, Giselle, and Brenda bake 111 muffins. Giselle bakes twice as many muffins as Brenda. Ellen bakes 9 fewer muffins than Giselle. How many muffins does Ellen bake?

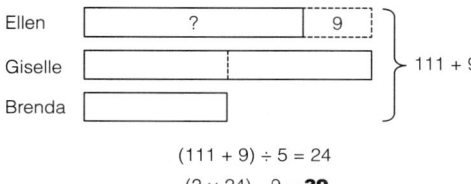

(111 + 9) ÷ 5 = 24
(2 × 24) − 9 = **39**

8. The model that involves sharing

There are 183 tennis balls in Basket A and 97 tennis balls in Basket B. How many tennis balls must be transferred from Basket A to Basket B so that both baskets contain the same number of tennis balls?

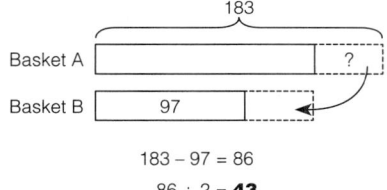

183 − 97 = 86
86 ÷ 2 = **43**

9. The model that involves fractions

George had 355 marbles. He lost $\frac{1}{5}$ of the marbles and gave $\frac{1}{4}$ of the remaining marbles to his brother. How many marbles did he have left?

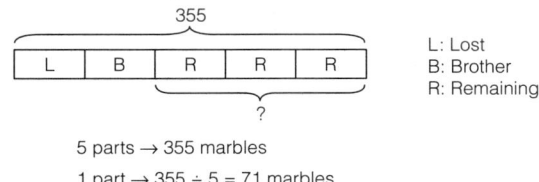

L: Lost
B: Brother
R: Remaining

5 parts → 355 marbles
1 part → 355 ÷ 5 = 71 marbles
3 parts → 3 × 71 = **213** marbles

10. The model that involves ratio

Aaron buys a tie and a belt. The prices of the tie and belt are in the ratio 2 : 5. If both items cost $539,
(a) what is the price of the tie?
(b) what is the price of the belt?

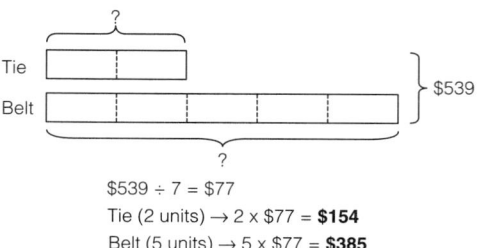

$539 ÷ 7 = $77
Tie (2 units) → 2 × $77 = **$154**
Belt (5 units) → 5 × $77 = **$385**

11. The model that involves comparison of fractions

Jack's height is $\frac{2}{3}$ of Leslie's height. Leslie's height is $\frac{3}{4}$ of Lindsay's height. If Lindsay is 160 cm tall, find Jack's height and Leslie's height.

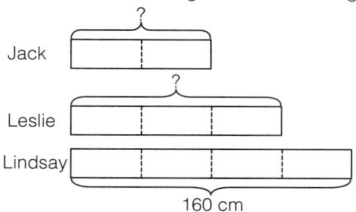

1 unit → 160 ÷ 4 = 40 cm
Leslie's height (3 units) → 3 × 40 = **120 cm**
Jack's height (2 units) → 2 × 40 = **80 cm**

Thinking skills and strategies are important in mathematical problem solving. These skills are applied when students think through the math problems to solve them. Below are some commonly used thinking skills and strategies applied in mathematical problem solving.

1. Comparing

Comparing is a form of thinking skill that students can apply to identify similarities and differences.

When comparing numbers, look carefully at each digit before deciding if a number is greater or less than the other. Students might also use a number line for comparison when there are more numbers.

Example:

3 is greater than 2 but smaller than 7.

2. Sequencing

A sequence shows the order of a series of numbers. *Sequencing* is a form of thinking skill that requires students to place numbers in a particular order. There are many terms in a sequence. The terms refer to the numbers in a sequence.

To place numbers in a correct order, students must first find a rule that generates the sequence. In a simple math sequence, students can either add or subtract to find the unknown terms in the sequence.

Example: Find the 7th term in the sequence below.

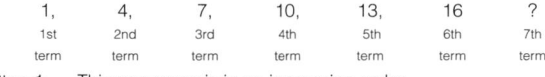

Step 1: This sequence is in an increasing order.
Step 2: 4 − 1 = 3   7 − 4 = 3
The difference between two consecutive terms is 3.
Step 3: 16 + 3 = 19
The 7th term is **19**.

3. Visualization

Visualization is a problem solving strategy that can help students visualize a problem through the use of physical objects. Students will play a more active role in solving the problem by manipulating these objects.

The main advantage of using this strategy is the mobility of information in the process of solving the problem. When students make a wrong step in the process, they can retrace the step without erasing or canceling it.

The other advantage is that this strategy helps develop a better understanding of the problem or solution through visual objects or images. In this way, students will be better able to remember how to solve these types of problems.

Some of the commonly used objects for this strategy are toothpicks, straws, cards, strings, water, sand, pencils, paper, and dice.

4. Look for a Pattern

This strategy requires the use of observational and analytical skills. Students have to observe the given data to find a pattern in order to solve the problem. Math word problems that involve the use of this strategy usually have repeated numbers or patterns.

Example: Find the sum of all the numbers from 1 to 100.

Step 1: <u>Simplify the problem.</u>
Find the sum of 1, 2, 3, 4, 5, 6, 7, 8, 9, and 10.

Step 2: <u>Look for a pattern.</u>
1 + 10 = 11   2 + 9 = 11   3 + 8 = 11
4 + 7 = 11   5 + 6 = 11

Step 3: <u>Describe the pattern.</u>
When finding the sum of 1 to 10, add the first and last numbers to get a result of 11. Then, add the second and second last numbers to get the same result. The pattern continues until all the numbers from 1 to 10 are added. There will be 5 pairs of such results. Since each addition equals 11, the answer is then 5 × 11 = 55.

Step 4: <u>Use the pattern to find the answer.</u>
Since there are 5 pairs in the sum of 1 to 10, there should be (10 × 5 = 50 pairs) in the sum of 1 to 100.
Note that the addition for each pair is not equal to 11 now. The addition for each pair is now (1 + 100 = 101).
50 × 101 = 5050
The sum of all the numbers from 1 to 100 is **5,050**.

5. Working Backward

The strategy of working backward applies only to a specific type of math word problem. These word problems state the end result, and students are required to find the total number. In order to solve these word problems, students have to work backward by thinking through the correct sequence of events. The strategy of working backward allows students to use their logical reasoning and sequencing to find the answers.

Example: Sarah has a piece of ribbon. She cuts the ribbon into 4 equal parts. Each part is then cut into 3 smaller equal parts. If the length of each small part is 35 cm, how long is the piece of ribbon?
3 × 35 = 105 cm
4 × 105 = 420 cm
The piece of ribbon is **420 cm**.

6. The Before-After Concept

The *Before-After* concept lists all the relevant data before and after an event. Students can then compare the differences and eventually solve the problems. Usually, the Before-After concept and the mathematical model go hand in hand to solve math word problems. Note that the Before-After concept can be applied only to a certain type of math word problem, which trains students to think sequentially.

Example: Kelly has 4 times as much money as Joey. After Kelly uses some money to buy a tennis racquet, and Joey uses $30 to buy a pair of pants, Kelly has twice as much money as Joey. If Joey has $98 in the beginning,
(a) how much money does Kelly have in the end?
(b) how much money does Kelly spend on the tennis racquet?

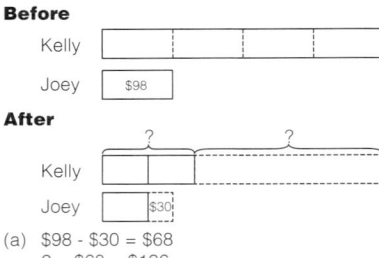

(a) $98 − $30 = $68
2 × $68 = $136
Kelly has **$136** in the end.
(b) 4 × $98 = $392
$392 − $136 = $256
Kelly spends **$256** on the tennis racquet.

7. Making Supposition

Making supposition is commonly known as "making an assumption." Students can use this strategy to solve certain types of math word problems. Making assumptions will eliminate some possibilities and simplifies the word problems by providing a boundary of values to work within.

Example: Mrs. Jackson bought 100 pieces of candy for all the students in her class. How many pieces of candy would each student receive if there were 25 students in her class?

In the above word problem, assume that each student received the same number of pieces. This eliminates the possibilities that some students would receive more than others due to good behaviour, better results, or any other reason.

8. Representation of Problem

In problem solving, students often use representations in the solutions to show their understanding of the problems. Using representations also allow students to understand the mathematical concepts and relationships as well as to manipulate the information presented in the problems. Examples of representations are diagrams and lists or tables.

Diagrams allow students to consolidate or organize the information given in the problems. By drawing a diagram, students can see the problem clearly and solve it effectively.

A list or table can help students organize information that is useful for analysis. After analyzing, students can then see a pattern, which can be used to solve the problem.

9. Guess and Check

One of the most important and effective problem-solving techniques is *Guess and Check*. It is also known as *Trial and Error*. As the name suggests, students have to guess the answer to a problem and check if that guess is correct. If the guess is wrong, students will make another guess. This will continue until the guess is correct.

It is beneficial to keep a record of all the guesses and checks in a table. In addition, a *Comments* column can be included. This will enable students to analyze their guess (if it is too high or too low) and improve on the next guess. Be careful; this problem-solving technique can be tiresome without systematic or logical guesses.

Example: Jessica had 15 coins. Some of them were 10-cent coins and the rest were 5-cent coins. The total amount added up to $1.25. How many coins of each kind were there?

Use the guess-and-check method.

Number of 10¢ Coins	Value	Number of 5¢ Coins	Value	Total Number of Coins	Total Value
7	7 × 10¢ = 70¢	8	8 × 5¢ = 40¢	7 + 8 = 15	70¢ + 40¢ = 110¢ = $1.10
8	8 × 10¢ = 80¢	7	7 × 5¢ = 35¢	8 + 7 = 15	80¢ + 35¢ = 115¢ = $1.15
10	10 × 10¢ = 100¢	5	5 × 5¢ = 25¢	10 + 5 = 15	100¢ + 25¢ = 125¢ = $1.25

There were **ten** 10-cent coins and **five** 5-cent coins.

10. Restate the Problem

When solving challenging math problems, conventional methods may not be workable. Instead, restating the problem will enable students to see some challenging problems in a different light so that they can better understand them.

The strategy of restating the problem is to "say" the problem in a different and clearer way. However, students have to ensure that the main idea of the problem is not altered.

How do students restate a math problem?

First, read and understand the problem. Gather the given facts and unknowns. Note any condition(s) that have to be satisfied.

Next, restate the problem. Imagine narrating this problem to a friend. Present the given facts, unknown(s), and condition(s). Students may want to write the "revised" problem. Once the "revised" problem is analyzed, students should be able to think of an appropriate strategy to solve it.

11. Simplify the Problem

One of the commonly used strategies in mathematical problem solving is simplification of the problem. When a problem is simplified, it can be "broken down" into two or more smaller parts. Students can then solve the parts systematically to get to the final answer.

Table of Contents

Introduction to Singapore Math..3

Learning Outcomes...9

Formula Sheet 10

Unit 9:   Decimals (Part 1)...13

Unit 10:   Decimals (Part 2)..27

Review 1 38

Unit 11:   Time...42

Unit 12:   Perimeter and Area 54

Review 2 68

Unit 13:   Symmetry 75

Unit 14:   Tessellations..82

Review 3 93

Final Review 101

Challenge Questions 112

Solutions 115

Singapore Math Practice Level 4B

LEARNING OUTCOMES

Unit 9 Decimals (Part 1)
Students should be able to
- recognize place values (tenths, hundredths, and thousandths) in decimals.
- express a fraction as a decimal, and vice versa.
- compare and arrange decimals.
- round decimals to the nearest whole number, 1 decimal place, or 2 decimal places.

Unit 10 Decimals (Part 2)
Students should be able to
- add and subtract decimals.
- multiply and divide decimals.
- estimate the value of decimals.
- check that answers are reasonable.
- solve up to 2-step story problems related to decimals.

Review 1
This review tests students' understanding of Units 9 & 10.

Unit 11 Time
Students should be able to
- count time in seconds.
- write time by separating hours, minutes, and seconds by a colon.
- find the length of 2 different times.
- calculate the starting or ending time given the length of time.

Unit 12 Perimeter and Area
Students should be able to
- calculate perimeter and area of rectangles, squares, and composite figures.
- find length or width of a rectangle/square given its perimeter/area.
- solve story problems related to perimeter and area.

Review 2
This review tests students' understanding of Units 11 & 12.

Unit 13 Symmetry
Students should be able to
- identify symmetrical figures.
- identify the lines of symmetry in figures.
- complete symmetrical figures and patterns.

Unit 14 Tessellations
Students should be able to
- identify shapes that repeat without gaps or overlaps.
- identify the unit shape in tessellations.
- complete tessellations by drawing more unit shapes on dot papers.
- draw unit shapes in tessellations in more than one way.

Review 3
This review tests students' understanding of Units 13 & 14.

Final Review
This review is an excellent assessment of students' understanding of all the topics in this book.

Singapore Math Practice Level 4B

FORMULA SHEET

Unit 9   Decimals (Part 1)

Word	Decimal	Fraction	
1 tenth	0.1	$\frac{1}{10}$	10 tenths = 1 one
1 hundredth	0.01	$\frac{1}{100}$	100 hundredths = 1 one
1 thousandth	0.001	$\frac{1}{1,000}$	1,000 thousandths = 1 one

<u>Writing decimals</u>
14.925 is **1 ten 4 ones 9 tenths 2 hundredths 5 thousandths**.

<u>Place value</u>
Each digit in a decimal is in a different place and has a different value. The place value will help us identify the digit in a particular place such as thousands, hundreds, tens, ones, tenths, hundredths, or thousandths and its value.

Example: In 43.082,
the digit 3 is in the **ones** place.
the digit 2 stands for **2 thousandths** or **0.002**.
the value of the digit 8 is **0.08**.

<u>More than and Less than</u>
The term *more than* means addition (+).
The term *less than* means subtraction (–).

<u>Comparing decimals</u>
1. Compare the whole numbers (thousands, hundreds, tens, and ones) first.
2. Next, compare the tenths.
3. Then, compare the hundredths.
4. Finally, compare the thousandths.

<u>Order</u>
When arranging a set of decimals in order,
- determine if the order must begin with the greatest or the smallest,
- compare the place value of the decimals,
- arrange the decimals in the correct order.

<u>Rounding decimals</u>
To round a decimal to the nearest whole number, look at the digit in the tenths place.
If the digit in the tenths place is equal to or more than 5, round up to a higher number.
If the digit in the tenths place is less than 5, the whole number will remain as it is.
Examples: $4.7 \approx 5 \qquad 4.1 \approx 4$

To round a decimal to the nearest tenth or 1 decimal place, look at the digit in the hundredths place.
If the digit in the hundredths place is equal to or more than 5, round up to the nearest tenth.
If the digit in the hundredths place is less than 5, the digit in the tenths place will remain.
Examples: $4.76 \approx 4.8 \qquad 4.72 \approx 4.7$

To round a decimal to the nearest hundredth or 2 decimal places, look at the digit in the thousandths place.
If the digit in the thousandths place is equal to or more than 5, round up to the nearest hundredth.
If the digit in the thousandths place is less than 5, the digit in the hundredths place will remain.
Examples: $4.759 \approx 4.76 \qquad 4.783 \approx 4.78$

Alternatively, use a number line as a guide in rounding decimals.
Example:

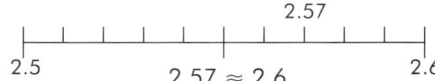

$2.57 \approx 2.6$

<u>Convert a fraction to a decimal</u>
Make the denominator 10, 100, or 1,000.
Remember to multiply both numerator and denominator with the same number.
Example: $\frac{1 \times 5}{20 \times 5} = \frac{5}{100} = 0.05$

<u>Convert a mixed number to a decimal</u>
- Break down the mixed number into a whole number and a fraction.
- Make the denominator 10, 100, or 1,000
- Convert the fraction to a decimal.

Example: $6\frac{3}{25} = 6 + \frac{3 \times 4}{25 \times 4} = 6 + \frac{12}{100} = 6\frac{12}{100} = 6.12$

<u>Convert a decimal to a fraction</u>
When a decimal has only tenths, the denominator is 10.
When a decimal has only hundredths, the denominator is 100.
When a decimal has only thousandths, the denominator is 1,000.
Example: $0.15 = \frac{15}{100}$

<u>Convert a decimal to a mixed number</u>
- Break down the decimal into a whole number and a decimal.
- Convert the decimal to a fraction.
- Add the fraction to the whole number.

- Write the fraction in its simplest form.

Example: $6.12 = 6 + 0.12 = 6 + \frac{12}{100} = 6\frac{12}{100} = 6\frac{3}{25}$

Unit 10 Decimals (Part 2)

Adding decimals
- Make sure the decimal points are aligned.
- Add the hundredths first. Regroup the tenths if required.
- Add the tenths. Regroup the tenths if required.
- Add the whole numbers. Regroup the whole numbers if required.

Subtracting decimals
- Make sure the decimal points are aligned.
- Subtract the hundredths first. Regroup if required.
- Subtract the tenths. Regroup if required.
- Subtract the whole numbers. Regroup if required.

Multiplying decimals
- Multiply the hundredths by the multiplier. Regroup the hundredths if required.
- Multiply the tenths by the multiplier. Regroup the tenths if required.
- Multiply the whole number by the multiplier. Regroup if required.

Dividing decimals
- Divide the whole number by the divisor. Regroup the remainder if required.
- Divide the tenths by the divisor. Regroup the remainder if required.
- Divide the hundredths by the divisor. There can be a remainder sometimes.

Estimation in decimals

Step 1: Round the numbers to the nearest whole number, the nearest tenth, or the nearest hundredth.

Step 2: Add, subtract, multiply, or divide accordingly.

Unit 11 Time

Seconds

1 minute = 60 seconds

Unit of measurement: sec.

Each number on the clock is equivalent to 5 seconds. The second hand on the clock is usually longer than the hour and minute hands.

Example: When the second hand moves from 3 to 5 on the face of the clock, it means 2 × 5 sec. = 10 sec. has passed.

Time can be written by separating hour, minutes, and seconds with a colon.

Example: nine thirty-three and twelve seconds in the morning is 9:33:12 A.M.

You can use a time line to find the duration or a particular time.

Unit 12 Perimeter and Area

Square

A square has four equal sides.

Perimeter = 4 × Length

Area = Length × Length

Rectangle

A rectangle has two pairs of equal sides.

Perimeter = Length + Width + Length + Width

Area = Length × Width

Composite Figures

In order to find the area or perimeter of a composite figure, first separate the figure into rectangle(s) or square(s).

Finding the selected area in a figure

Area of shaded area = Area of big rectangle − Area of small rectangle

Unit 13 Symmetry

A *line of symmetry* is a line that divides a figure into two equal parts. The *line of symmetry* is usually a dotted line.

A symmetrical figure is a figure that can be divided into two equal parts by a line of symmetry.

Some examples of symmetrical figures:

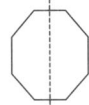 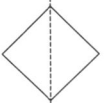 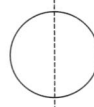

Completing symmetrical shapes or patterns

Step 1: Use the dotted line as the line of symmetry.

Step 2: Trace or shade the other half of the symmetrical shape or pattern accordingly to the first half.

Unit 14 Tessellations

A *tessellation* is a type of pattern that is tiled using a unit shape with no gaps in between.

Examples of tessellations:

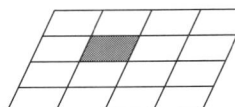 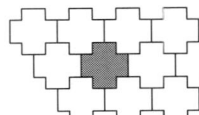

A tessellation can be made by using a unit shape on the dot grid. Also, tessellations can be drawn with some shapes in 2 or more ways.

Singapore Math Practice Level 4B

Unit 9: DECIMALS (PART 1)

Examples:

1. Change $8\frac{37}{100}$ to a decimal.

    $8\frac{37}{100}$ = 8 ones 37 hundredths = **8.37**

2. What number is 0.005 more than 6.323? **6.328**

    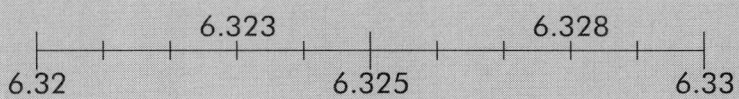

3. Arrange the decimals in order, beginning with the largest.

    0.708   0.078   0.78

    0.78, 0.708, 0.078

4. Round 28.69 to the nearest tenth.

    28.69 ≈ **28.7**

The shaded parts represent the decimals. Write the correct decimals on the lines provided.

1.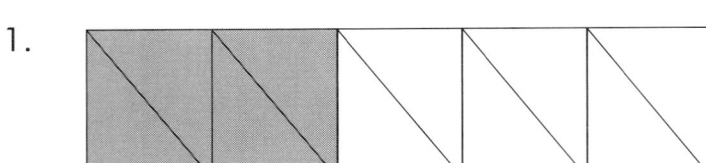

2.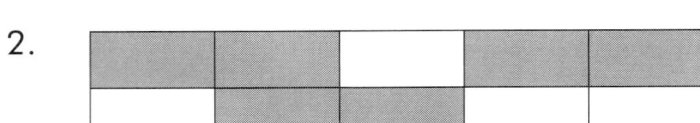

3.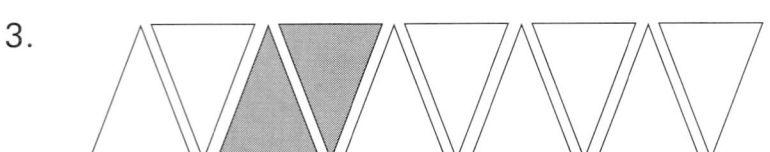

4.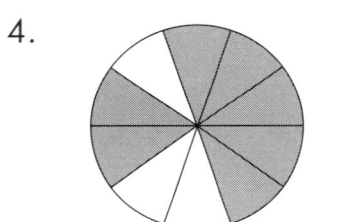

5.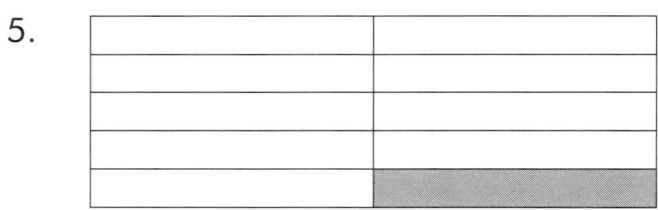

Write the following in decimals.

6. 7 tenths = _____

7. 3 ones 2 tenths = _____

8. 4 ones 13 tenths = _____

9. 2 ones 18 tenths = _____

10. 9 ones 24 tenths = _____

Write each decimal in tenths.

11. 0.9 = _____ tenths

12. 3.6 = _____ tenths

13. 78.4 = _____ tenths

14. 18.3 = _____ tenths

15. 21.5 = _____ tenths

For each number line, fill in each box with the correct decimal.

16.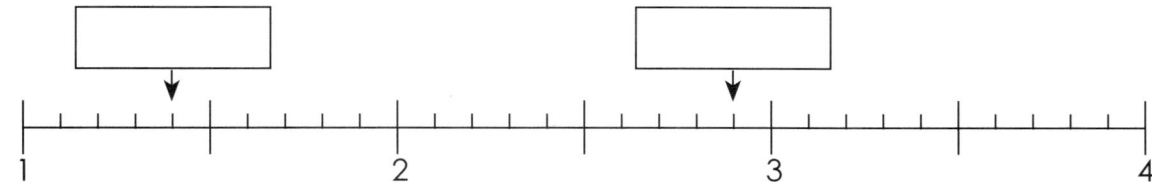

17.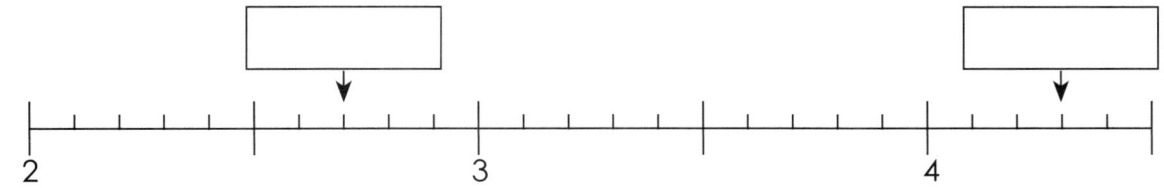

Singapore Math Practice Level 4B

18.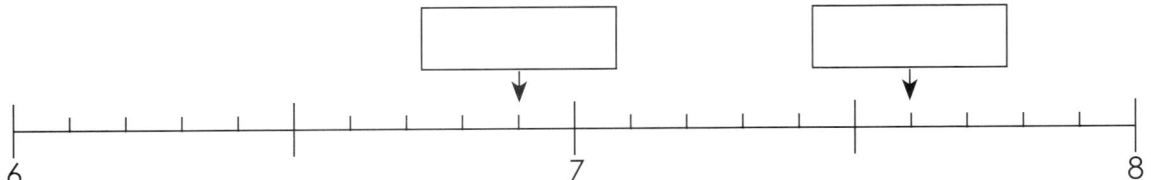

Fill in each blank with the correct answer.

19. 9.1 = _____ ones 1 tenth

20. 42.6 = _____ tens 2 ones 6 tenths

21. 17.3 = 1 ten 7 ones _____ tenths

22. 69.5 = _____ tens 9 ones 5 tenths

23. 82.8 = 8 tens 2 ones _____ tenths

24. In 91.3,

    (a) the digit _____ is in the ones place.

    (b) the digit 3 is in the _____ place.

    (c) the value of the digit 9 is _____.

    (d) the digit 1 stands for _____.

25. In 57.6,

    (a) the digit _____ is in the tens place.

    (b) the digit 6 is in the _____ place.

    (c) the value of the digit 7 is _____.

    (d) the digit 5 stands for _____.

For each question, shade the boxes accordingly to show the correct decimal.

26.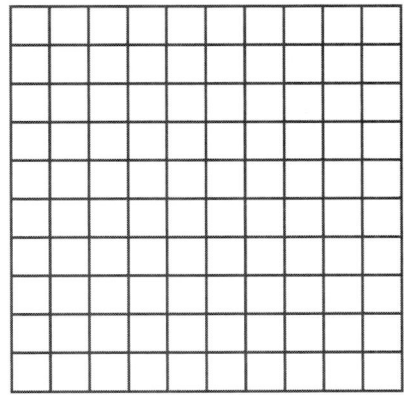

0.26

29.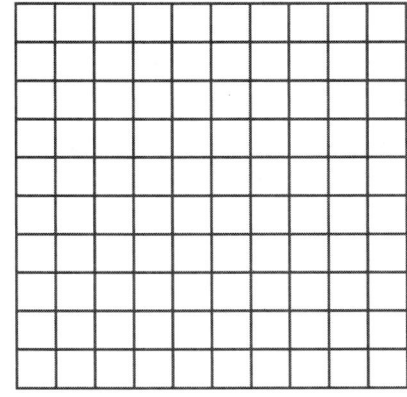

0.62

27.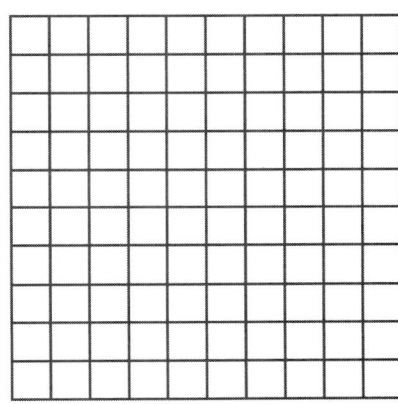

0.74

30.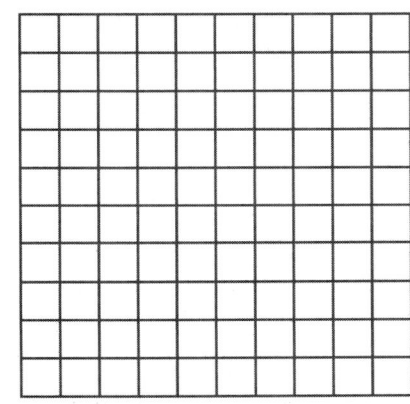

0.45

28.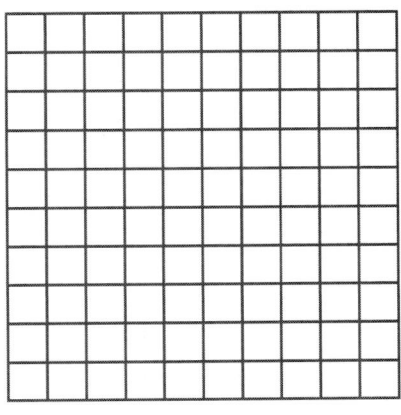

0.03

Write the following in decimals.

31. 8 hundredths = _____

32. 16 hundredths = _____

33. 32 hundredths = _____

34. 188 hundredths = _____

35. 311 hundredths = _____

Write each decimal in hundredths.

36. 5.43 = _____ hundredths

37. 81.95 = _____ hundredths

38. 60.72 = _____ hundredths

39. 38.54 = _____ hundredths

40. 90.45 = _____ hundredths

For each number line, fill in each box with the correct decimal.

41.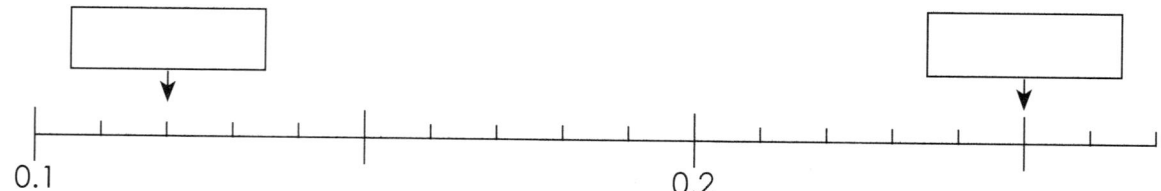

42.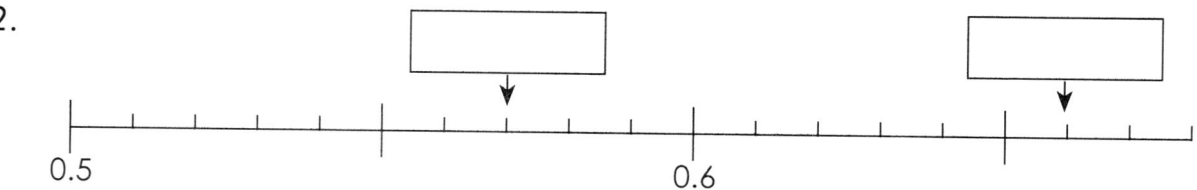

43.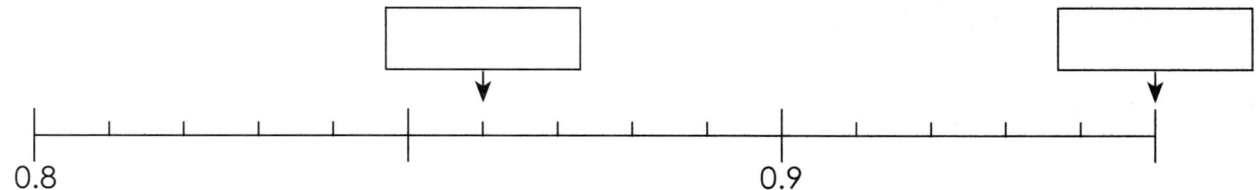

Fill in each blank with the correct answer.

44. 20.45 = _____ tens _____ ones _____ tenths _____ hundredths

45. 71.38 = _____ tens _____ one _____ tenths _____ hundredths

46. 94.28 = _____ tens _____ ones _____ tenths _____ hundredths

47. 64.13 = _____ tens _____ ones _____ tenth _____ hundredths

48. 52.56 = _____ tens _____ ones _____ tenths _____ hundredths

49. In 70.24,

   (a) the digit _____ is in the ones place.

   (b) the digit 7 is in the _____ place.

   (c) the digit 2 stands for _____.

   (d) the value of the digit 4 is _____.

   (e) the value of the digit 7 is _____.

50. In 93.18,

   (a) the digit _____ is in the tenths place.

   (b) the digit 9 is in the _____ place.

Singapore Math Practice Level 4B

(c) the digit 3 stands for _____.

(d) the value of the digit 8 is _____.

(e) the value of the digit 1 is _____.

Write the following in decimals.

51. 4 thousandths = _____

52. 15 thousandths = _____

53. 291 thousandths = _____

54. 718 thousandths = _____

55. 1,414 thousandths = _____

56. 2,086 thousandths = _____

Write each decimal in thousandths.

57. 28.404 = _____ thousandths

58. 40.687 = _____ thousandths

59. 53.936 = _____ thousandths

60. 2.308 = _____ thousandths

61. 66.799 = _____ thousandths

For each number line, fill in each box with the correct decimal.

62.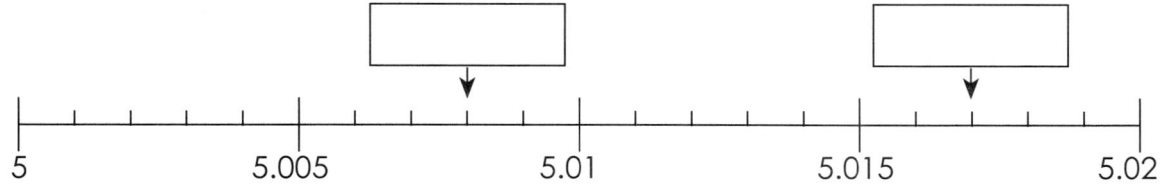

63.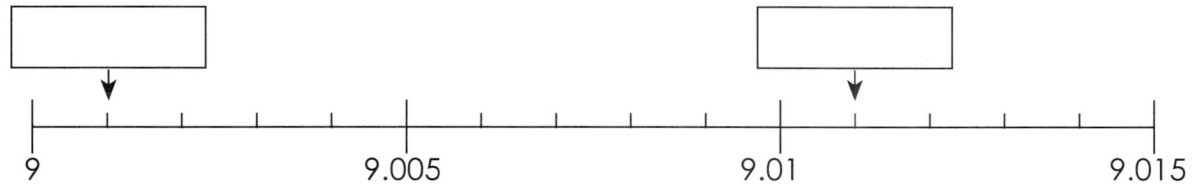

64.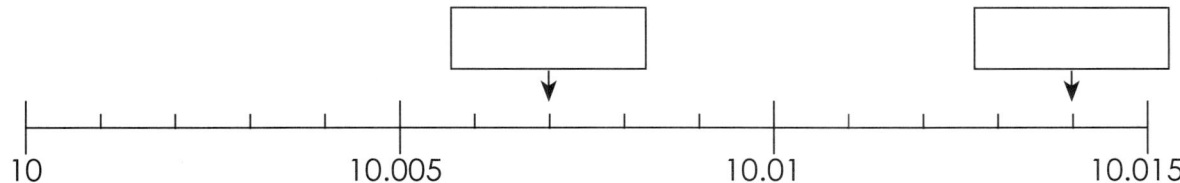

Fill in each blank with the correct answer.

65. 20.045 = _____ tens _____ ones _____ tenths _____ hundredths _____ thousandths

66. 58.297 = _____ tens _____ ones _____ tenths _____ hundredths _____ thousandths

67. 72.393 = _____ tens _____ ones _____ tenths _____ hundredths _____ thousandths

68. 36.816 = _____ tens _____ ones _____ tenths _____ hundredth _____ thousandths

69. 84.035 = _____ tens _____ ones _____ tenths _____ hundredths _____ thousandths

Singapore Math Practice Level 4B

70. In 4.687,

    (a) the digit _____ is in the thousandths place.

    (b) the digit 6 is in the _____ place.

    (c) the digit 8 stands for _____.

    (d) the value of the digit 7 is _____.

    (e) the value of the digit 4 is _____.

71. In 10.963,

    (a) the digit _____ is in the ones place.

    (b) the digit 3 is in the _____ place.

    (c) the digit 9 stands for _____.

    (d) the value of the digit 1 is _____.

    (e) the value of the digit 6 is _____.

72. 0.5 more than 13.9 is _____.

73. 0.02 more than 78.66 is _____.

74. 0.006 less than 85.09 is _____.

75. 0.2 less than 6.7 is _____.

76. 0.01 less than 57.03 is _____.

Complete the number patterns.

77. 3.8, 4.7, 5.6, _____, _____

78. 15.34, 15.39, 15.44, _____, _____

79. 45.06, 45.09, 45.12, _____, _____

80. 10.088, 10.089, 10.09, _____, _____

81. 82.309, 82.314, 82.319, _____, _____

Circle the largest decimal.

82.	1.28	1.028	1.8	1.208
83.	$3\frac{605}{1,000}$	3.65	3.506	$\frac{365}{1,000}$
84.	2.91	$2\frac{901}{1,000}$	$2\frac{9}{100}$	0.291

Circle the smallest decimal.

85.	7.102	7.12	7.021	7.012
86.	$8\frac{95}{100}$	8.095	8.905	$\frac{8,059}{1,000}$
87.	3.99	$3\frac{909}{1,000}$	$3\frac{99}{1,000}$	$\frac{399}{1,000}$

Arrange the decimals in descending order.

88. 5.028,   2.058,   5.28

_____

89. 4.25,   4.025,   4.502

_____

90. 1.09,   9.01,   0.19

_____

Arrange the decimals in ascending order.

91. 198.3,   198.03,   198.003

_____

92. 273.29,   27.329,   2,732.9

_____

93. 6.017,   6.17,   6.107

_____

Round the following decimals to the nearest whole numbers.

94. 1.04 _____

95. 2.55 _____

96. 15.82 _____

97. 0.95 _____

98. 7.74 _____

Round the following decimals to 1 decimal place.

99. 1.68 _____

100. 33.38 _____

101. 2.91 _____

Round the following decimals to the nearest tenth.

102. 14.74 _____

103. 6.472 _____

104. 89.943 _____

Round the following decimals to 2 decimal places.

105. 10.963 _____

106. 59.095 _____

107. 7.007 _____

Singapore Math Practice Level 4B

Round the following decimals to the nearest hundredths.

108.   0.671   _____

109.   2.386   _____

110.   15.709   _____

Write the following fractions as decimals.

111. $\frac{4}{10} =$ _____

112. $\frac{11}{10} =$ _____

113. $5\frac{8}{10} =$ _____

114. $9\frac{4}{5} =$ _____

115. $\frac{1}{100} =$ _____

116. $\frac{28}{100} =$ _____

117. $1\frac{77}{100} =$ _____

118. $4\frac{18}{25} =$ _____

119. $\frac{462}{1,000} =$ _____

120. $\frac{9}{1,000} =$ _____

121. $5\frac{16}{1,000} =$ _____

122. $45\frac{45}{50} =$ _____

Write each decimal as a fraction or a mixed number in its simplest form.

123.   6.2 = _____

124.   49.4 = _____

125.   7.08 = _____

126.   51.25 = _____

127.   1.008 = _____

128.   25.42 = _____

Unit 10: DECIMALS (PART 2)

Examples:

1. 3.28 + 4.05 = **7.33**

$$\begin{array}{r} \overset{1}{3}.28 \\ +\,4.05 \\ \hline 7.33 \end{array}$$

2. 5.94 − 2.31 = **3.63**

$$\begin{array}{r} 5.94 \\ -\,2.31 \\ \hline 3.63 \end{array}$$

3. 9.4 × 6 = **56.4**

$$\begin{array}{r} \overset{2}{9}.4 \\ \times\ \ \ 6 \\ \hline 56.4 \end{array}$$

4. 15.3 ÷ 5 = **3.06**

$$\begin{array}{r} 3.06 \\ 5\overline{)15.3} \\ \underline{15} \\ 3 \\ \underline{0} \\ 30 \\ \underline{30} \\ 0 \end{array}$$

5. Estimate 2.91 × 6.

  2.91 × 6 ≈ 3 × 6 = **18**

Singapore Math Practice Level 4B

Solve the addition problems below.

1.   0.1
    + 0.3
    ———

4.   5.14
    + 13.63
    ———

2.   6.2
    + 1.3
    ———

5.   56.01
    + 72.96
    ———

3.   9.08
    + 5.57
    ———

6.   39.78
    + 44.05
    ———

Solve the subtraction problems below.

7.   0.5
    −   0.2
    ―――――

8.   9.7
    −   5.4
    ―――――

9.   4.61
    −   2.39
    ―――――

10.   21.75
    −   8.03
    ―――――

11.   97.36
    − 50.72
    ―――――

12.   80.49
    − 31.67
    ―――――

Singapore Math Practice Level 4B

Solve the multiplication problems below.

13.   5 . 1
    ×   2
———

18.   3 . 4 5
    ×   3
———

14.   0 . 4
    ×   5
———

19.   0 . 7 8
    ×   9
———

15.   3 . 8
    ×   4
———

20.   1 2 . 3 6
    ×   5
———

16.   2 . 3
    ×   6
———

21.   5 0 . 1 2
    ×   2
———

17.   8 . 1 7
    ×   7
———

22.   2 1 . 5 5
    ×   6
———

Solve the division problems below.

23. $3\overline{)7.8}$

27. $9\overline{)27.45}$

24. $5\overline{)5.25}$

28. $4\overline{)43.4}$

25. $2\overline{)4.89}$

29. $9\overline{)812.7}$

26. $4\overline{)16.4}$

30. $6\overline{)402.15}$

31. 5)̄18

32. 8)̄10

33. Estimate the value of each of the following by first rounding the number to the nearest whole number. Then, decode the message below.

A 26.54 + 92.88 = _____

C 84.05 − 77.13 = _____

D 5.4 × 8 = _____

E 11.99 ÷ 3 = _____

I 125.09 + 68.01 = _____

L 524.87 − 128.39 = _____

M 44.19 × 5 = _____

S 35.59 ÷ 6 = _____

40	4	7	193	220	120	397	6

Singapore Math Practice Level 4B

Solve the following story problems. Show your work in the space below.

34. Mrs. Abdul bought 2.4 lb. of meat. Mrs. Davidson bought 1.35 lb. of meat more than her. How many pounds of meat did they buy altogether?

35. Joan had $108.25. She spent $43.05 to buy a present for her mother and $12.20 on cab fare. How much money did she have left?

36. A bag of rice and two identical bags of sugar have a mass of 6 kg. The bag of rice and a bag of sugar have a mass of 4.5 kg. Find the mass of five bags of sugar.

37. A train traveled 180.63 mi. on Monday. It traveled 2.1 mi. more on Tuesday than on Monday. It traveled 1.2 mi. less on Wednesday than on Tuesday. What was the distance traveled by the train on Wednesday?

38. Lily has a mass of 24.3 kg. The mass of her father is 3 times as heavy as Lily. What is the total mass of Lily and her father?

39. A ribbon is 21.75 yd. long. Wang cuts two pieces of ribbon measuring a total of 2.4 yd. from it. The remaining piece of ribbon is then cut into three equal pieces. What is the length of each of the three pieces of ribbon?

Singapore Math Practice Level 4B

40. A box of chocolates cost $11.45. Marcus bought three boxes of chocolates. If he gave the cashier a fifty-dollar bill, how much change would he receive?

41. Mr. Mendoza needed 12.76 gal. of paint to paint a room.
    (a) How much paint would he need if he wanted to paint three similar rooms?
    (b) If a gallon of paint cost $5, how much money did Mr. Jackson pay for the paint?

42. Mr. Woods had a bag of sugar. He sold 38.25 kg of it and packed the rest equally into six bags. If each bag of sugar had a mass of 0.75 kg, how much sugar did Mr. Woods have in the beginning?

43. Taylor bought 2 bottles of orange juice and a bottle of apple juice for $6.55. The bottle of apple juice cost $0.35 less than the bottle of orange juice. What was the cost of the bottle of orange juice?

REVIEW 1

Choose the correct answer. Write its number in the parentheses.

1. In 372.48, the digit 8 is in the _____ place.
   (1) ones (3) hundredths
   (2) tenths (4) thousandths   ( )

2. Express $\frac{2}{5}$ as a decimal.
   (1) 0.25 (3) 0.5
   (2) 0.4 (4) 2.5   ( )

3. Find the sum of 5.98 and 1.93.
   (1) 4.05 (3) 7.91
   (2) 6.39 (4) 8.91   ( )

4. Express 62.458 in thousandths.
   (1) 624.58 thousandths (3) 62,458 thousandths
   (2) 6,245.8 thousandths (4) 624,580 thousandths   ( )

5. Round 37.46 to 1 decimal place.
   (1) 37.0 (3) 37.5
   (2) 37.4 (4) 38.0   ( )

6. 288.63 ÷ 9 = _____
   (1) 3.207 (3) 32.7
   (2) 32.07 (4) 320.7   ( )

7. Estimate the value of 12.99 + 5.5 by rounding each number to the nearest whole number first.
   (1) 17
   (2) 18
   (3) 19
   (4) 20
   ( )

Write your answers on the lines.

8. 5 hundreds, 4 tens, 7 tenths, and 1 thousandth written in numerals is ☐.

9. Write 1.68 as a mixed number in its simplest form.

10. In 89.437, the value of the digit 4 is ☐.

11. $9\frac{35}{100} = 9 +$ ☐

    Write your answer in decimal.

12. Jar A contains 1.9 gallons of water. Jar B contains 2.1 gallons of water and Jar C contains 1.2 gallons of water. What is the total volume of water in the three jugs? Write your answer as a decimal.

13. Find the product of 1.92 and 8. Round your answer to the nearest tenth.

14. 305.419 = 3 hundreds 5 ones 4 tenths ☐ thousandths

Singapore Math Practice Level 4B

15. Arrange the following decimals in descending order.

    5.06   0.56   5.6   5.006

    _____

16. Katrina has a ribbon 3.78 m long. The length of her ribbon is 3 times as long as Sarah's ribbon. How much longer is Katrina's ribbon than Sarah's ribbon?

    _____

17. Mrs. Cho bought 2.76 lb. of grapes and divided the grapes equally among three neighbors and herself. How much did each person get?

    _____

Solve the following story problems. Show your work in the space below.

18. Elsie travels 12.9 mi. from her house to her office every day. She travels the same distance back home. What is the total distance traveled by Elsie from Monday to Friday?

19. A boutique paid $2,954.10 to its supplier for 12 similar dresses and 7 similar blouses. If all the dresses cost $2,376.60, how much did each blouse cost?

20. Sheila used 3.6 m of cloth from a 10-m cloth to sew two similar blouses. The remaining cloth was used to sew four identical skirts. How much cloth did Sheila use to sew each skirt?

Unit 11: TIME

Examples:

1. Draw the missing minute and second hands on the clock shown on the right.

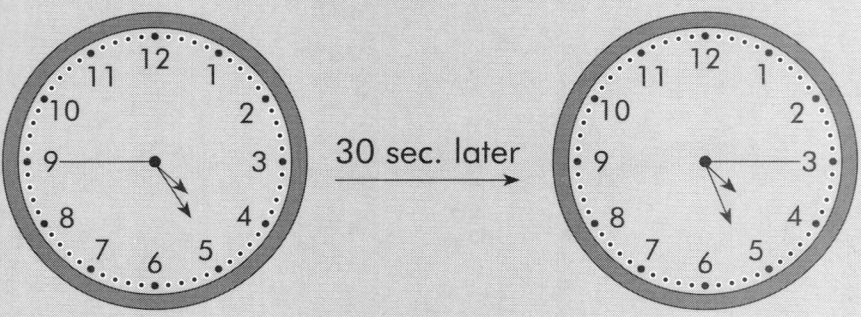

2. Write the time two thirty and twenty-five seconds in the afternoon by separating hours, minutes, and seconds with a colon.

   2:30:25 P.M.

3. Noel started reading a book at 12:56 P.M. She finished reading the book at 2:05 P.M. How long did she use to read the book?

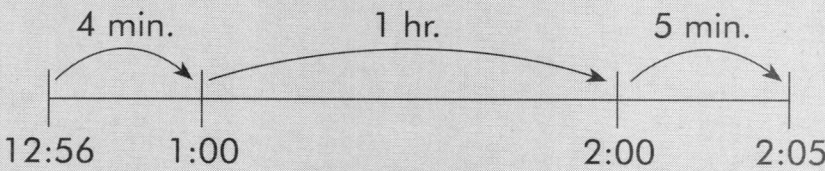

   1 hr. + 4 min. + 5 min. = 1 hr. 9 min.

   She used **1 hr. 9 min.** to read the book.

Write the correct length of time on the lines.

1.

   James took _____ sec. to get out of his bed.

2.

   James took _____ sec. to wash his hands.

3.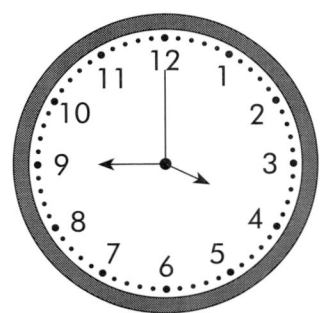

   James took _____ sec. to walk from his room to the kitchen.

Singapore Math Practice Level 4B

4.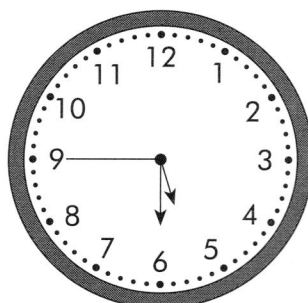

James took _____ sec. to pick a piece of paper from the floor.

5.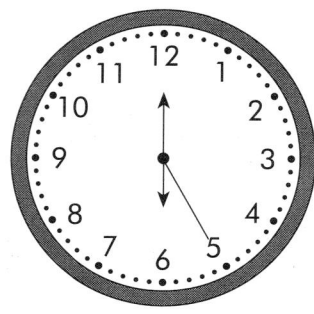

James took _____ sec. to wash his spoon and fork at the basin.

Draw the missing minute and second hands on each clock shown on the right.

6. Leyla used 40 sec. to read a sentence in her book.

7. Angie used 20 sec. to draw an apple.

8. Andre used 60 sec. to walk to the garden.

9. Jessica used 15 sec. to color a square.

10. Leo used 55 sec. to wash two plates.

 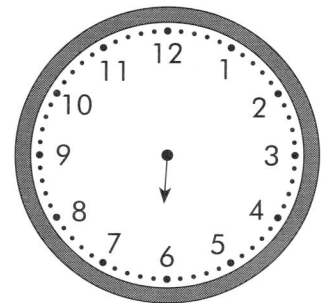

Write the expected time.

11. It is 5:34:21 P.M.

    What time will it be in 1 hr. 3 min. 45 sec.? _____

12. It is 10:55:47 A.M.

    What time will it be in 2 hr. 6 min. 34 sec.? _____

13. It is 8:20:39 P.M.

    What time will it be in 8 hr. 19 min. 54 sec.? _____

14. It is 6:41:36 A.M.

    What time will it be in 7 hr. 49 min. 20 sec.? _____

15. It is 12:02:59 P.M.

    What time will it be in 0 hr. 59 min. 59 sec.? _____

Singapore Math Practice Level 4B

Write the elapsed time.

16. It is 11:27:06 A.M.

    What time was it 6 hr. 42 min. 42 sec. ago? _____

17. It is 3:28:15 P.M.

    What time was it 4 hr. 22 min. 10 sec. ago? _____

18. It is 7:19:21 A.M.

    What time was it 10 hr. 11 min. 8 sec. ago? _____

19. It is 10:44:30 P.M.

    What time was it 5 hr. 53 min. 25 sec. ago? _____

20. It is 2:08:16 A.M.

    What time was it 3 hr. 39 min. 14 sec. ago? _____

For each time line, fill in each blank with the correct answer.

21.
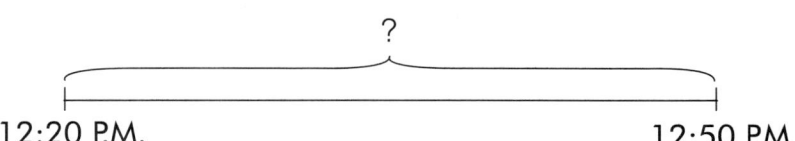

Mindy took _____ to travel from the library to her house.

22.
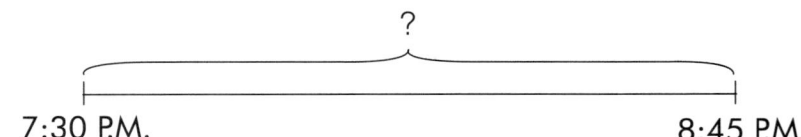

Isra's piano lesson lasted _____.

Singapore Math Practice Level 4B

23.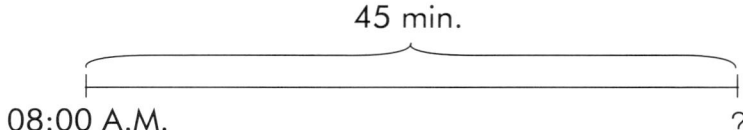

Peggy finished her swimming lesson at _____.

24.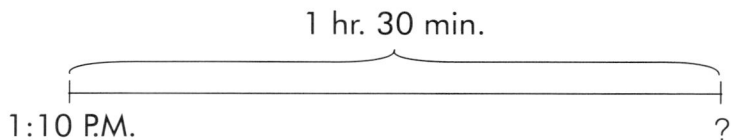

The television program ended at _____.

25.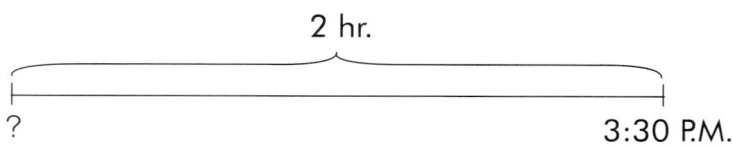

Jerome took a nap at _____.

26.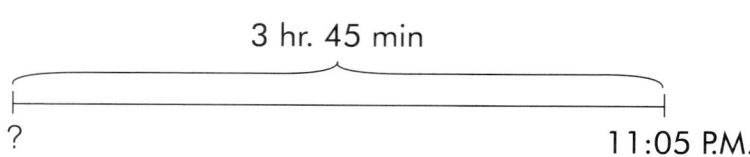

Wendy started studying at _____.

Solve the following story problems. Show your work in the space below.

27. Mike started doing his project at 5:15 P.M. He finished his project at 8:30 P.M. How long did he take to do his project?

28. The time shown on Basil's watch is 3:20 P.M. If his watch is 30 minutes fast, what should be the correct time?

Singapore Math Practice Level 4B

29. Benjamin reached his grandmother's house at 1:40 P.M. If the trip from his house to his grandmother's house took 25 min., at what time did Benjamin leave his house?

30. Mrs. Murray went to a shopping center at 4:00 P.M. She finished her shopping at 5:45 P.M. How long did she spend at the shopping center?

31. A concert lasted 3 hr. 15 min. If the concert ended at 11:55 P.M., at what time did the concert start?

32. The time it takes for a plane to fly from Boston to Washington, D.C. is 90 min. If the plane leaves Boston at 12:40 P.M., at what time will the plane reach Washington, D.C.?

33. An exam started at 8:05 A.M. It lasted 2 hr. 30 min. At what time did the exam end?

34. A coach traveled from Town X to Town Y. The coach started the trip at 10:35 P.M. and reached Town Y at 7:15 A.M. the next morning. How long was the trip?

35. When it is 9:30 P.M. in New York, the clock in San Francisco shows 12:30 P.M. If the time in San Francisco is 4 P.M., what time is it in New York?

Unit 12: PERIMETER AND AREA

Examples:

1. The area of a rectangular paper is 90 cm². Its length is 10 cm. Find its width.

    Area = Length × Width
    90 cm² = 10 cm × Width
    Width = 90 ÷ 10 = 9 cm

   Its width is **9 cm**.

2. The perimeter of a square is 36 in. Find its area.

    Perimeter = 4 × Length
    36 in. = 4 × Length
    Length = 36 ÷ 4 = 9 in.

    Area = Length × Length
    = 9 × 9
    = 81 in.²

   Its area is **81 in.²**.

3. Find the area of the figure below.

    Area of square = 10 × 10
    = 100 ft.²

    Area of rectangle = 15 × 62
    = 930 ft.²

    100 + 930 = 1,030 ft.²

   The area of the figure is **1,030 ft.²**.

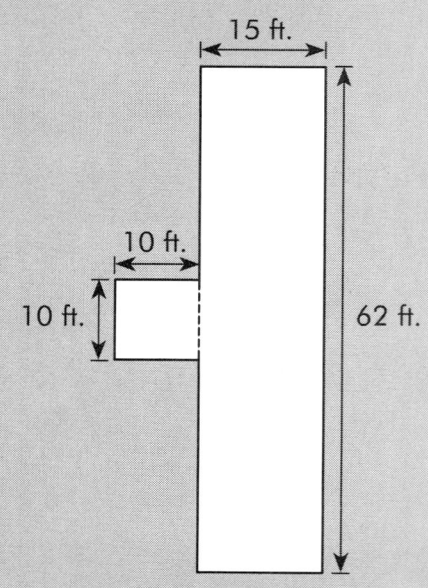

54

Singapore Math Practice Level 4B

Find the perimeter and area of each figure.

1.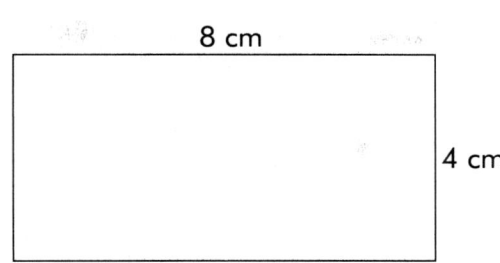

   Perimeter of rectangle = _____ + _____ + _____ + _____

   = _____ cm

   Area of rectangle = _____ × _____

   = _____ cm²

2.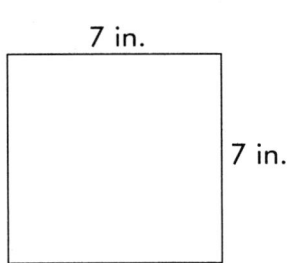

   Perimeter of square = _____ + _____ + _____ + _____

   = _____ in.

   Area of square = _____ × _____

   = _____ in.²

3.

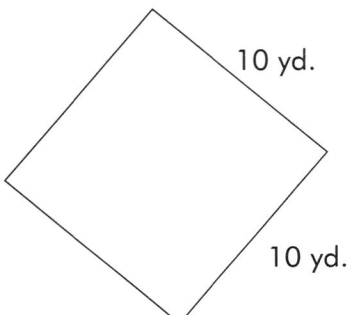

Perimeter of square = _____ + _____ + _____ + _____

= _____ yd.

Area of square = _____ × _____

= _____ yd.²

4.

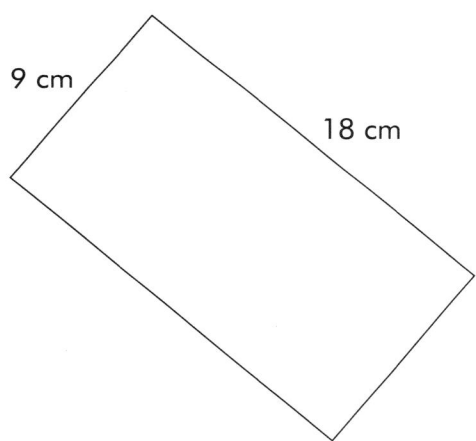

Perimeter of rectangle = _____ + _____ + _____ + _____

= _____ cm

Area of rectangle = _____ × _____

= _____ cm²

5.

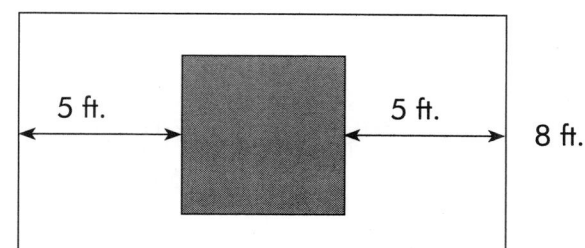

Perimeter of rectangle = _____ + _____ + _____ + _____

= _____ ft.

Area of square = _____ × _____

= _____ ft.^{2}

Solve the problems below. Write your answers on the lines.

6. The perimeter of a rectangle is 44 in. If the width of the rectangle is 5 in., what is its length?

_____

7. The perimeter of a square is 52 cm. Find its length. _____

8. The area of a rectangle is 36 cm². Find the length of the rectangle if its width is 4 cm.

_____

9. The perimeter of a rectangle is 52 yd. Find its width if its length is 15 yd.

_____

Singapore Math Practice Level 4B

10. The area of a square is 81 ft.². Find its length. _____

11. The area of a square table is 64 cm². Find the perimeter of the square table.

    _____

12. The perimeter of a rectangle is 48 in. If the length of the rectangle is two times its width, what is the area of the rectangle?

    _____

13. The perimeter of a table is 6 ft. If the width is 1 ft., find its area.

    _____

14. The area of a square room is 16 m². Find the perimeter of the room.

    _____

15. The area of a rectangular field is 150 yd.². If its length is $1\frac{1}{2}$ times its width, find the perimeter of the field.

    _____

16. The figure below is made up of two rectangles. Find its perimeter.

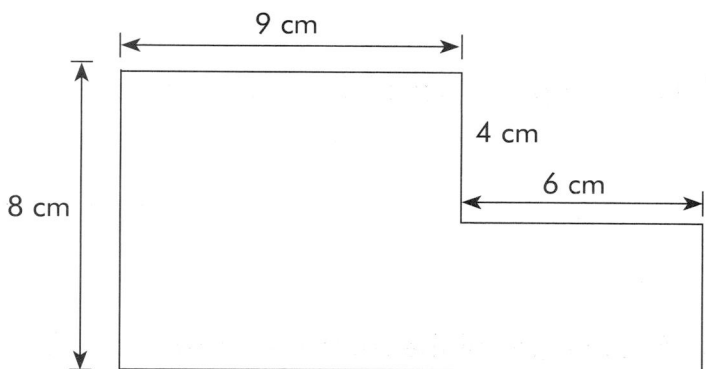

17. The figure below is made up of a square and two rectangles. Find its area.

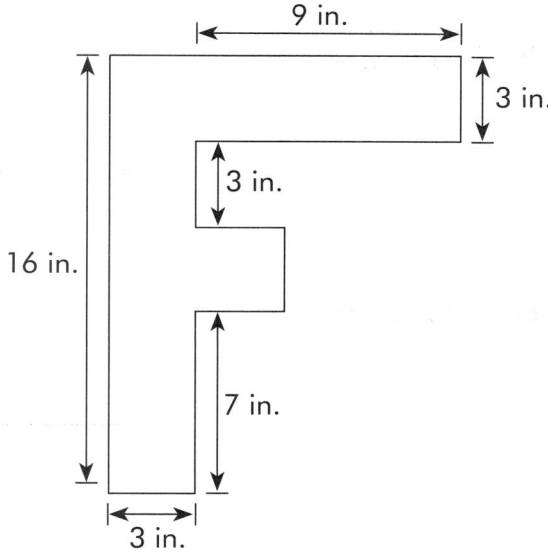

18. The figure below is made up of three rectangles. Find its area and perimeter.

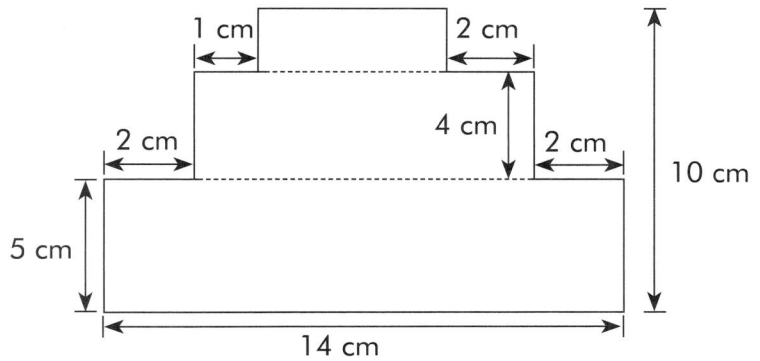

Area = _____

Perimeter = _____

Singapore Math Practice Level 4B

19. Find the area and perimeter of the figure below.

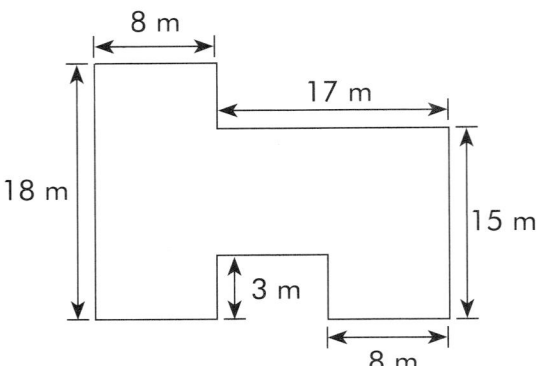

Area = _____

Perimeter = _____

20. Find the area and perimeter of the figure below.

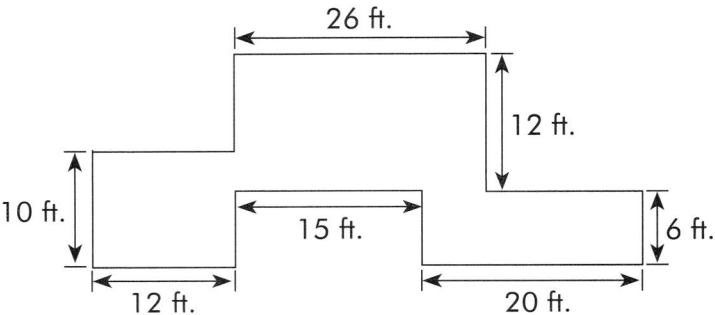

Area = _____

Perimeter = _____

Solve the following story problems. Show your work in the space below.

21. The figure below shows the floor plan of Rita's house. How big is her house?

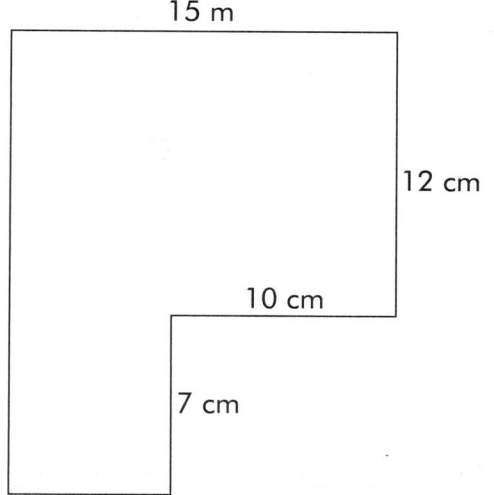

22. The figure below shows an exhibition hall. Part of the exhibition hall is covered with carpet. Find the area that is covered with carpet.

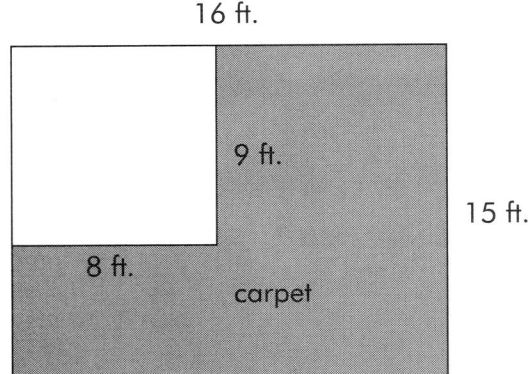

23. The figure below is made up of six identical squares of a total area of 294 cm². Find the perimeter of the shaded portion.

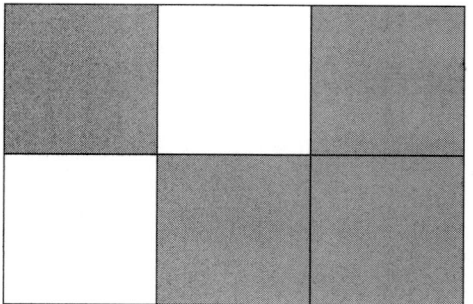

24. A white rectangular board measuring 28 in. long and 16 in. wide is placed in the center of a larger rectangular board. It creates a border of 3 in. around it. Find the area not covered by the white rectangular board.

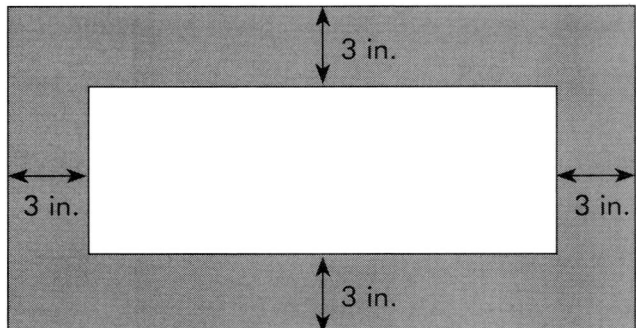

25. Mary's room measures 8 m by 7 m. If the area not covered by carpet measures 4.5 m by 4 m, find the floor area in her room that is covered by carpet.

26. A farmer had a plot of land measuring 15 yd. by 11 yd. The farmer put up a fence, leaving a margin of 2 yd. wide all round it.

   (a) Find the length of the fence.

   (b) If the fence cost $3.85 a yard, how much did it cost to put a fence round the plot of land?

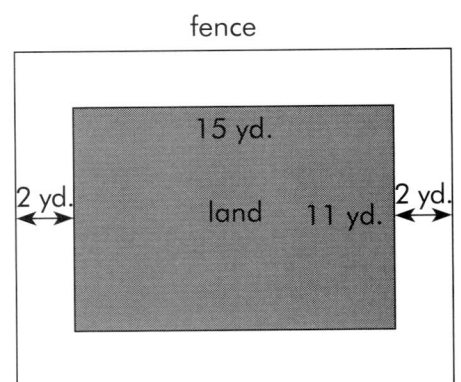

27. Tammy bought a square cardboard. She cut a letter "L" from the cardboard as shown below. Find the remaining area of the cardboard.

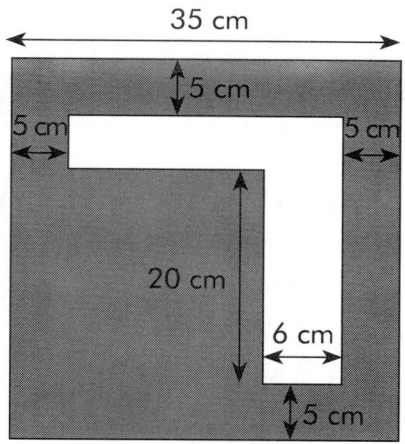

REVIEW 2

Choose the correct answer. Write its number in the parentheses.

1. The length of a rectangle is 32 in. Its length is twice its width. What is the perimeter of the rectangle?

    (1) 48 in.   (3) 192 in.

    (2) 96 in.   (4) 512 in.   ( )

2. Which of the following shows ten fifty-five and thirty-six seconds at night?

    (1) 10.55.36 P.M.   (3) 1055:36 P.M.

    (2) 10:55:36 P.M.   (4) 10.55:36 P.M.   ( )

3. The length of a square field is 256 m. Paul ran 6 times around the field. Find the total distance that he ran.

    (1) 1,024 m   (3) 4,096 m

    (2) 1,536 m   (4) 6,144 m   ( )

The clocks below show the length of time Brian takes to type a sentence.

4. How many seconds does Brian take to type the sentence?

   (1) 4
   (2) 20
   (3) 30
   (4) 40   (   )

5. The perimeter of the figure below is _____.

   (1) 36 ft.
   (2) 42 ft.
   (3) 48 ft.
   (4) 51 ft.

   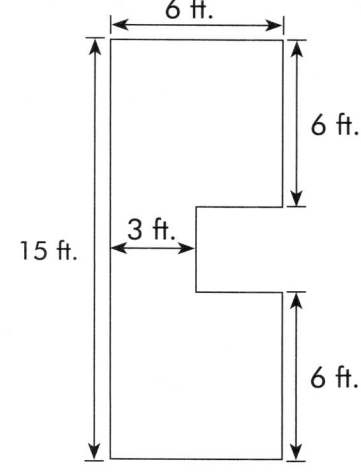

   (   )

6. The perimeter of a rectangle is 64 cm. If its length is 19 cm, find its width.

   (1) 13 cm
   (2) 15 cm
   (3) 22.5 cm
   (4) 26 cm   (   )

7. Jeremy started practicing for his piano recital at 4:40 P.M. He stopped at 6:15 P.M. How long did he practice for his piano recital?

   (1) 1 hr. 45 min.
   (2) 1 hr. 35 min.
   (3) 1 hr. 25 min.
   (4) 1 hr. 15 min.   (   )

Write your answers on the lines.

8. A square has a perimeter of 40 yd. What is its area?

   _____

Singapore Math Practice Level 4B

9. The figure below is made of 3 rectangles. Find the area of the figure.

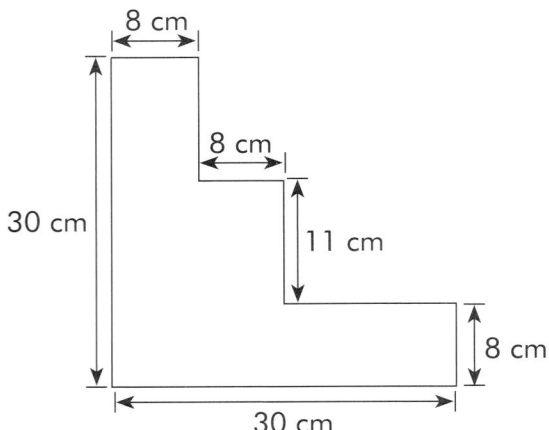

10. The figure is made up of 4 identical squares. It has an area of 256 ft.^{2}. What is the length of each square?

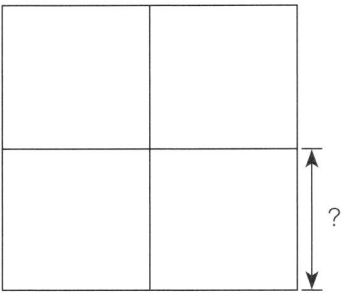

11. The figure below is made up of a square and a rectangle. Square A and Rectangle B have the same area. What is the perimeter of the figure?

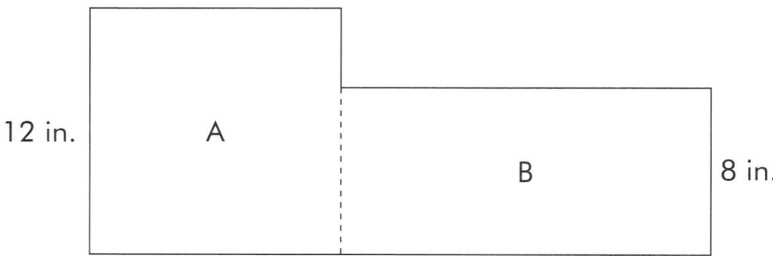

12. Find the area of the shaded part.

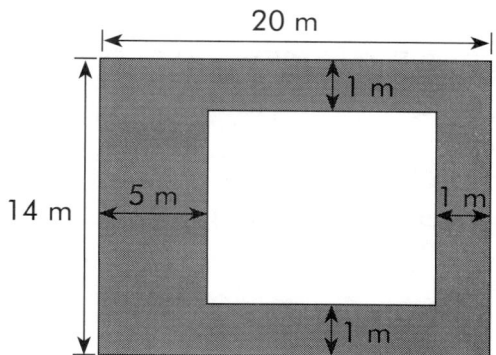

13. Kisha started her school lessons at 7:45 A.M. Her lessons lasted for 5 hr. 30 min. What time did her lessons end?

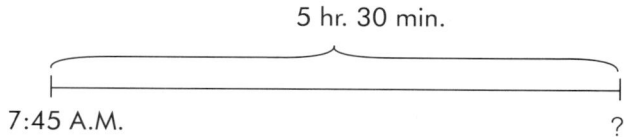

14. Write the time ten twenty-two and forty-three seconds at night. _____

15. Mandy used 40 sec. to peel an apple. Draw the correct second hand on the clock shown on the right.

Singapore Math Practice Level 4B

Solve the following story problems. Show your work in the space below.

16. Mr. Edmonds wants to tile a 2-foot wide pavement around a swimming pool measuring 15 ft. by 12 ft.

    (a) Find the area of pavement Mr. Edmonds needs to tile.

    (b) How much does he have to pay if the tile costs $29 per square foot?

17. Mr. Simon works from 9:30 P.M. every night. He will stop work at 7:55 A.M. the next day. How long does he work every night?

18. In the figure, X and Z are identical squares. Y is a bigger square. The area of square X is 49 cm² and the area of square Y is 81 cm². What is the perimeter of the figure?

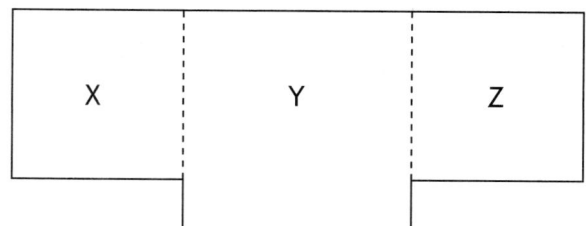

19. Phil has a piece of cardboard of length 120 in. Its width is $\frac{3}{5}$ as long as its length. Find the area of the cardboard.

20. When it is 7:00 A.M. in Denver, the clock in London, England shows 2:00 P.M. If Jennifer wants to call her mother who is in London at 8:00 P.M., at what time should she make the call in Denver?

Unit 13: SYMMETRY

Examples:

1. Which of the following figures are symmetrical?

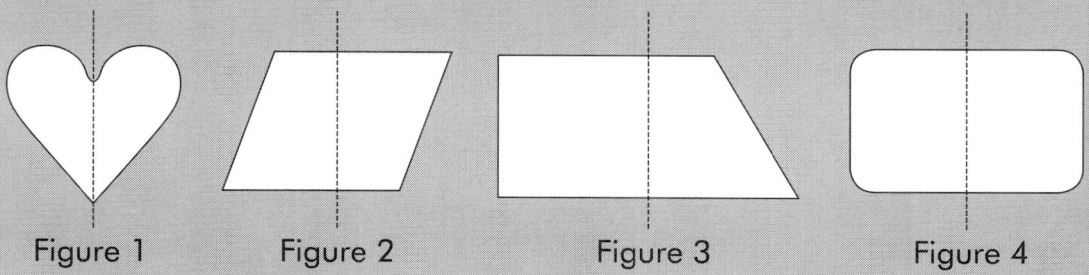

Figure 1   Figure 2   Figure 3   Figure 4

Figures __1__ and __4__ are symmetrical.

2. Complete the symmetrical pattern below.

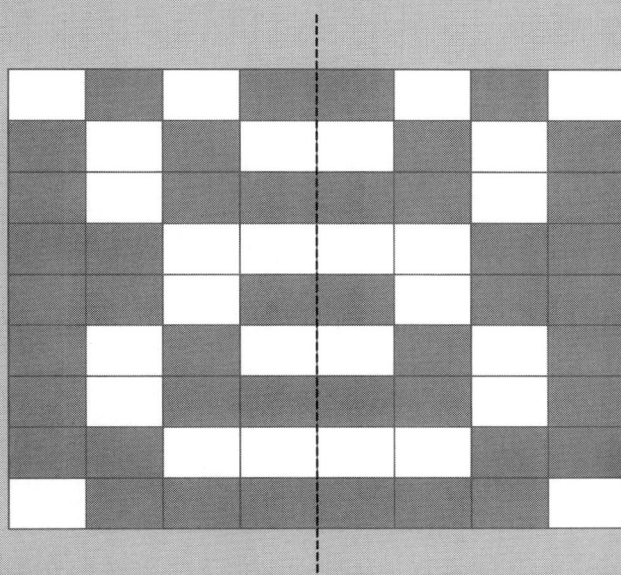

Singapore Math Practice Level 4B

Some of the letters shown below are symmetrical. Write Yes in the blank if the letter is symmetrical and write No in the blank if the letter is not symmetrical.

1. A _____

2. M _____

3. O _____

4. D _____

5. E _____

6. F _____

7. G _____

8. H _____

9. L _____

Study each figure carefully. Write *Yes* in the blank if the dotted line is a line of symmetry or *No* in the blank if the dotted line is not a line of symmetry.

10.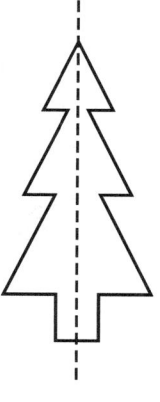

_____

13.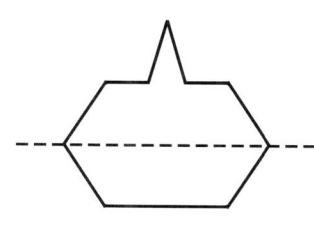

_____

11.

_____

14.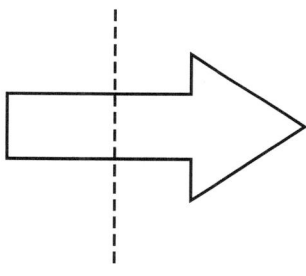

_____

12.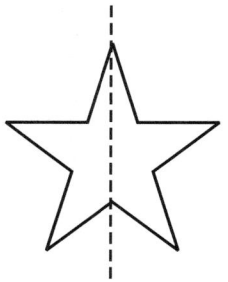

_____

15.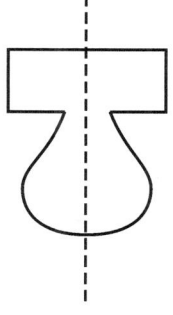

_____

Singapore Math Practice Level 4B

Complete the symmetrical figures.

16.

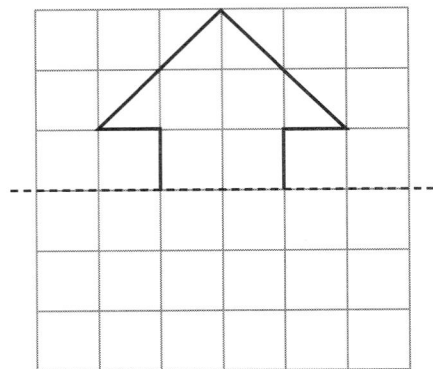

17.

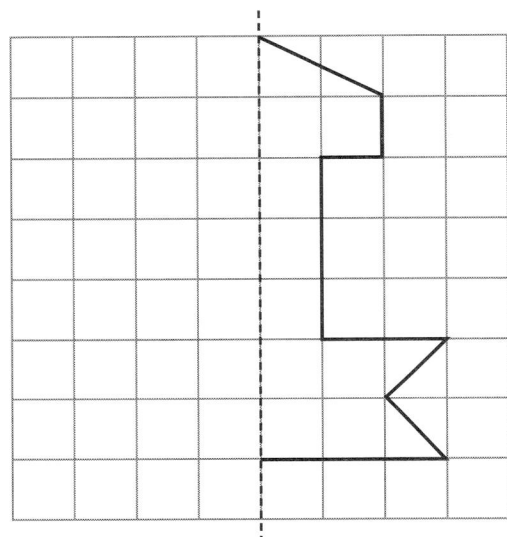

18.

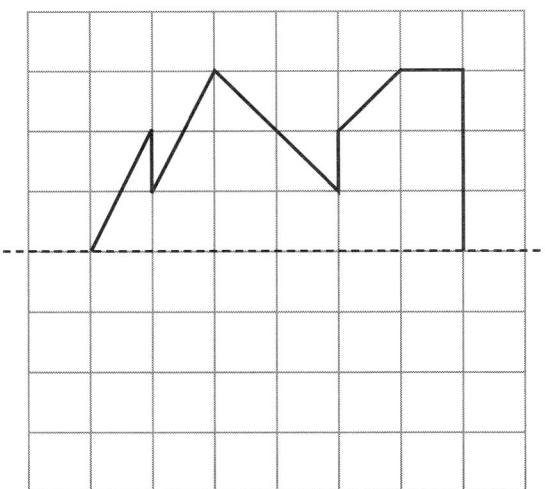

19.

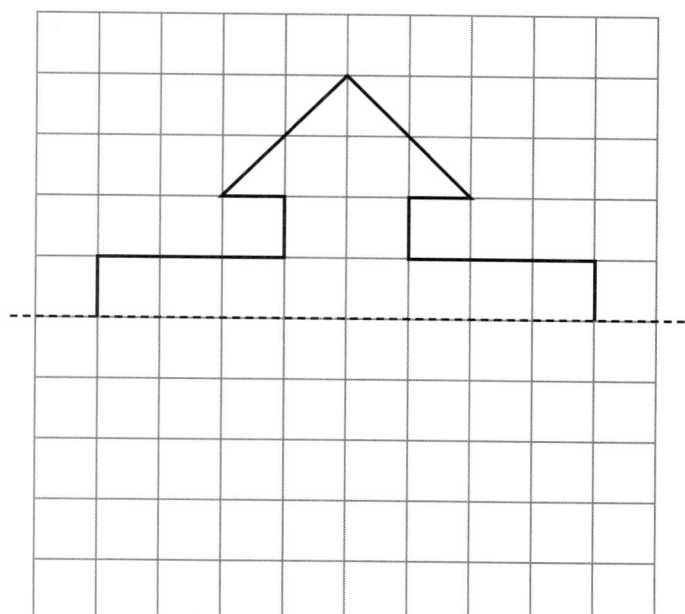

20.

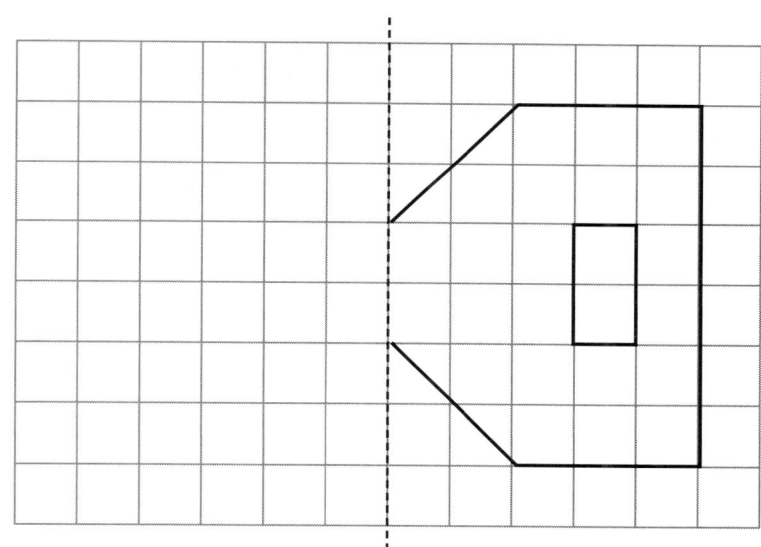

21.

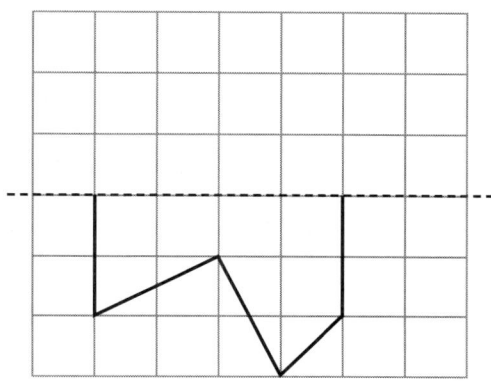

Singapore Math Practice Level 4B

Complete the symmetrical patterns.

22.

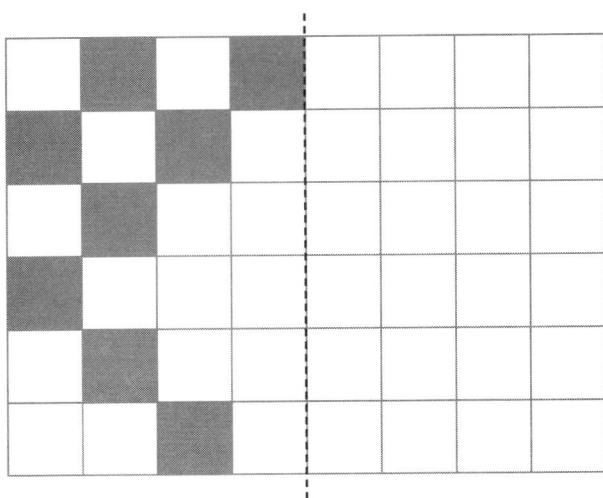

23.

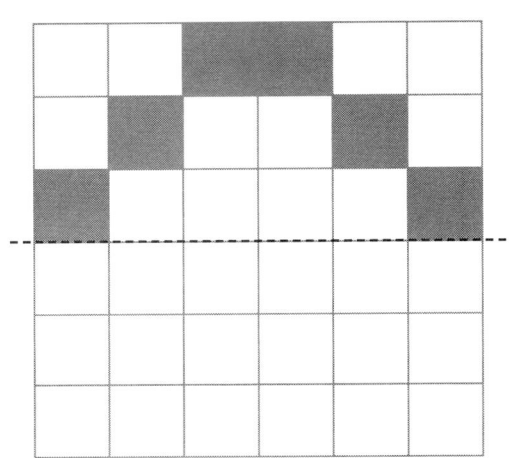

24.

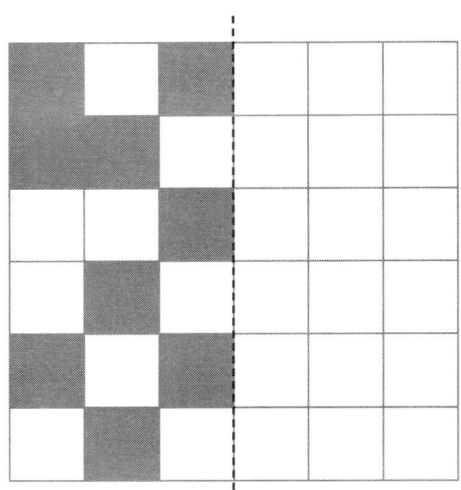

25.

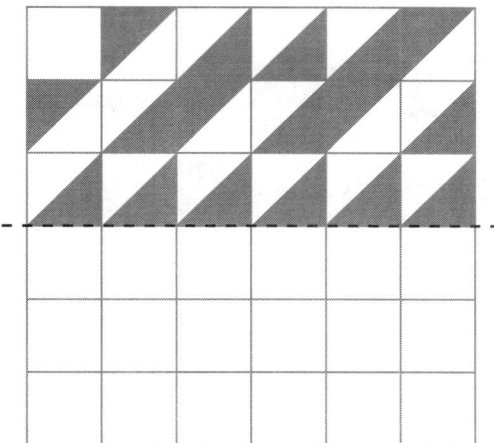

26.

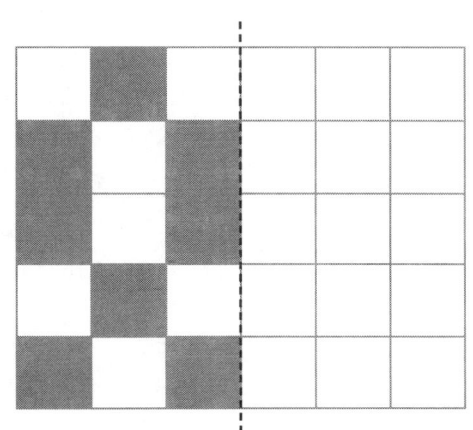

27.

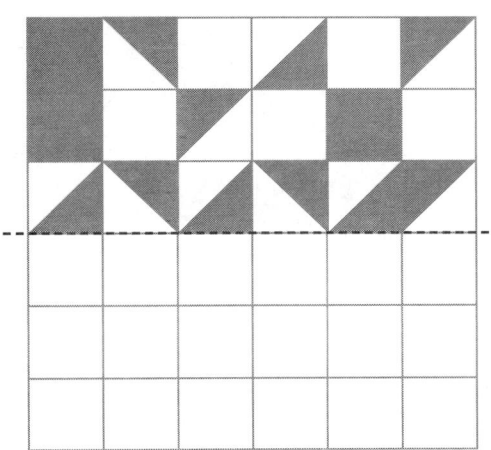

Unit 14: TESSELLATIONS

Examples:

1. Identify the unit shape in the tessellation below.

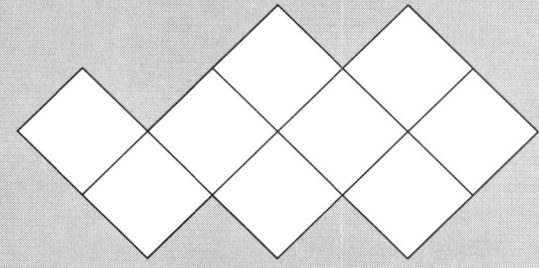

The unit shape is ◇.

2. Make a tessellation of the unit shape by adding 8 more unit shapes.

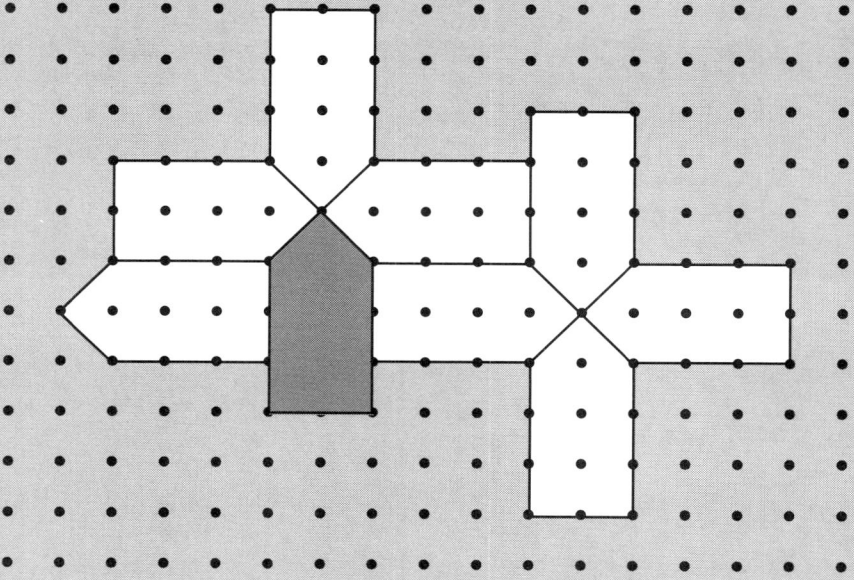

For each tessellation, identify the unit shape by shading it.

1.

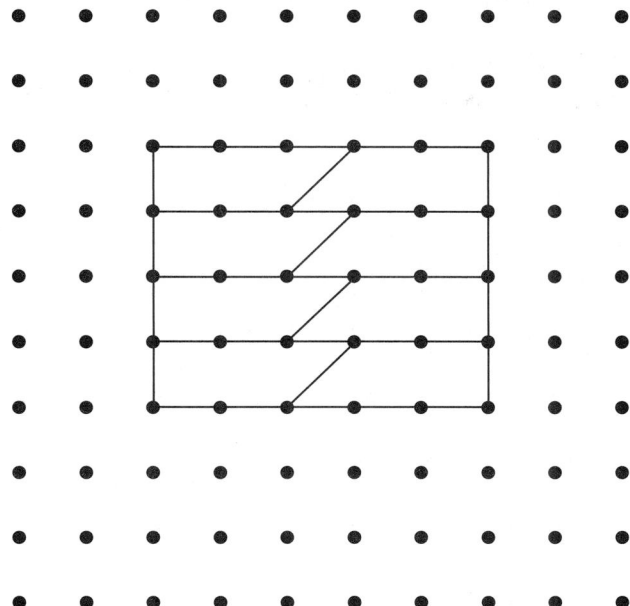

2.

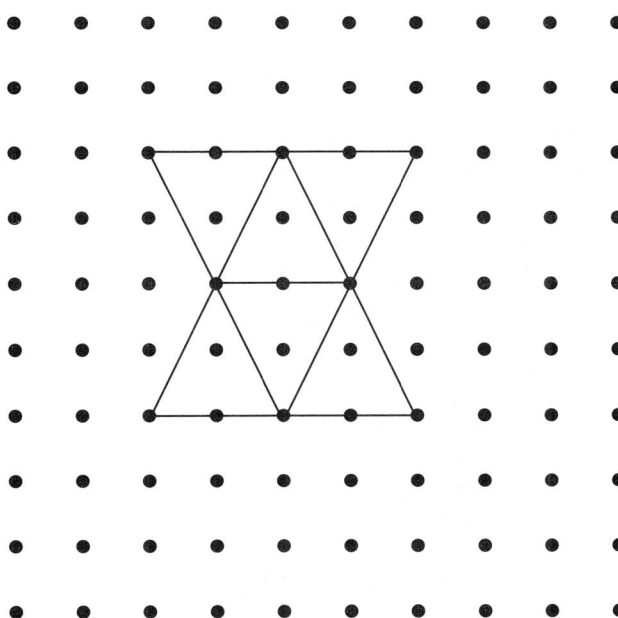

3.

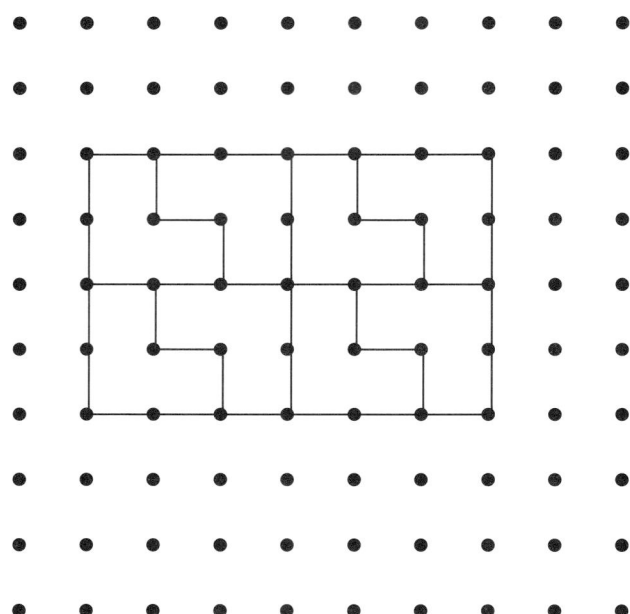

4.

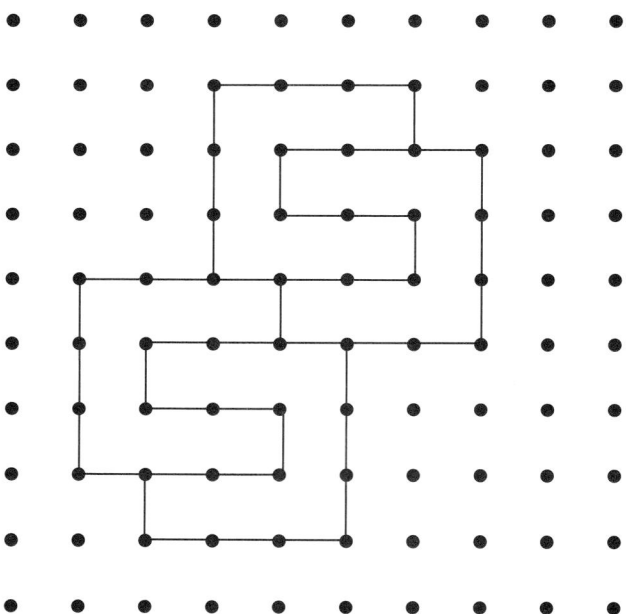

5.

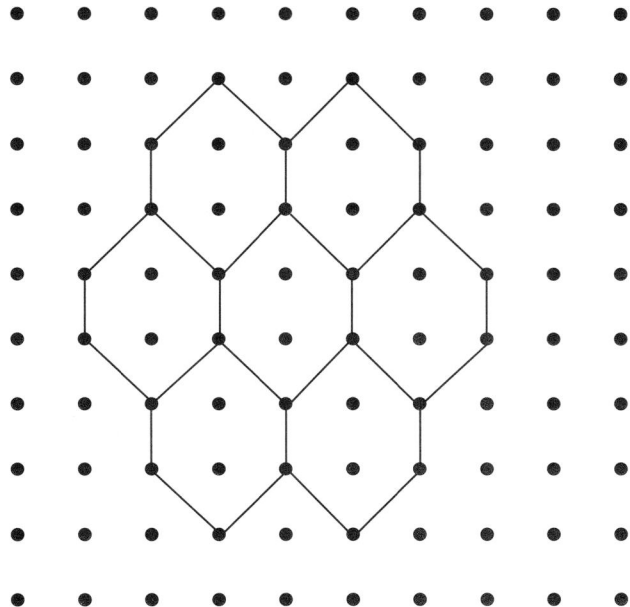

State if the following shapes tessellate or repeat without gaps or overlaps. Write Yes in the blank if it tessellates or No if it does not tessellate.

6.

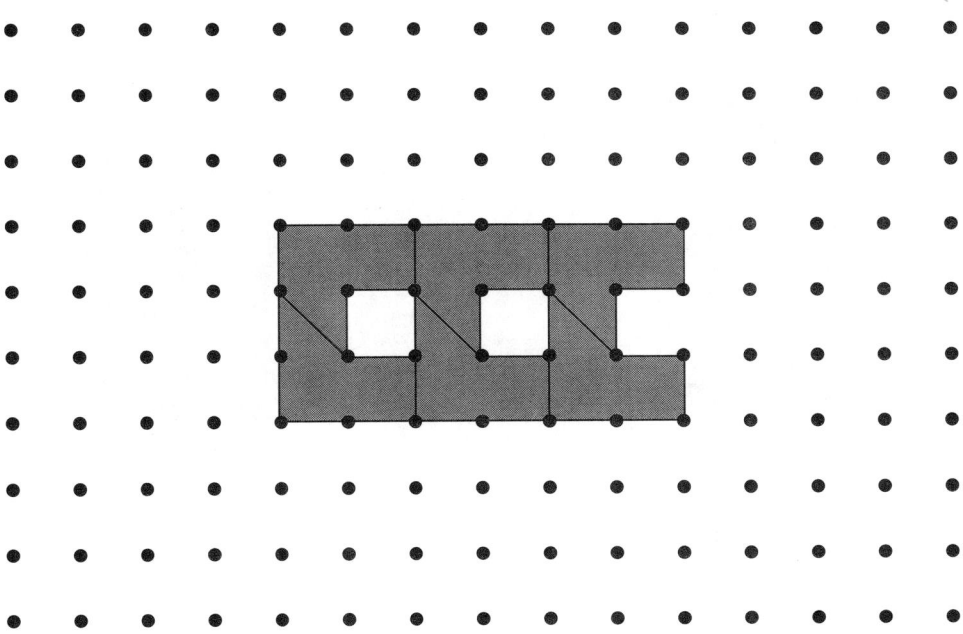

7.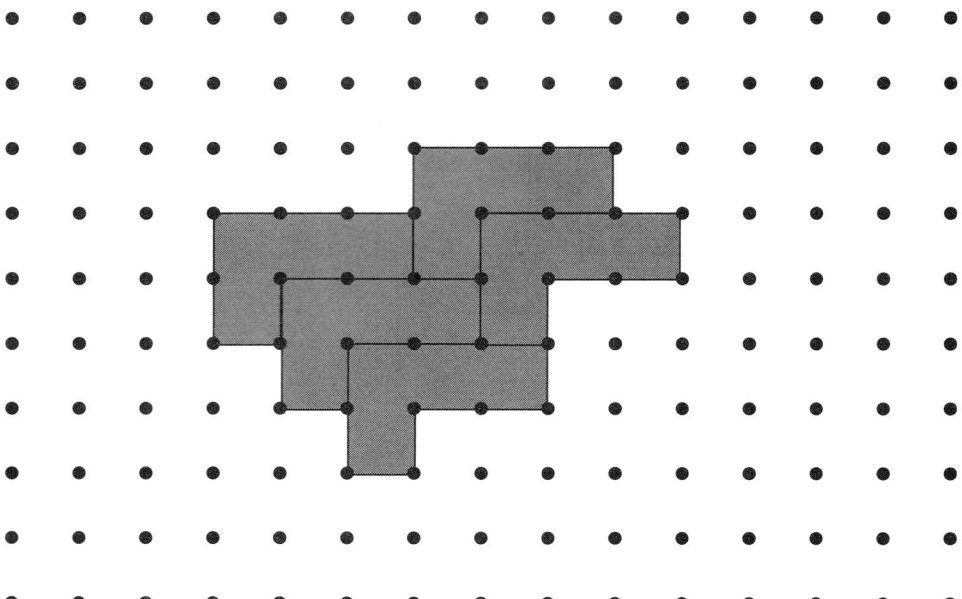

8.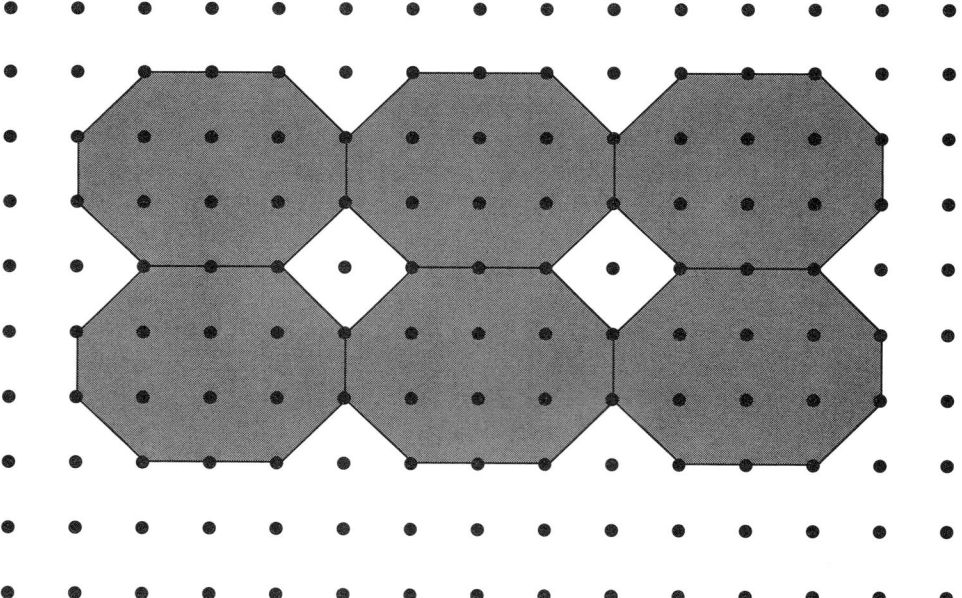

9.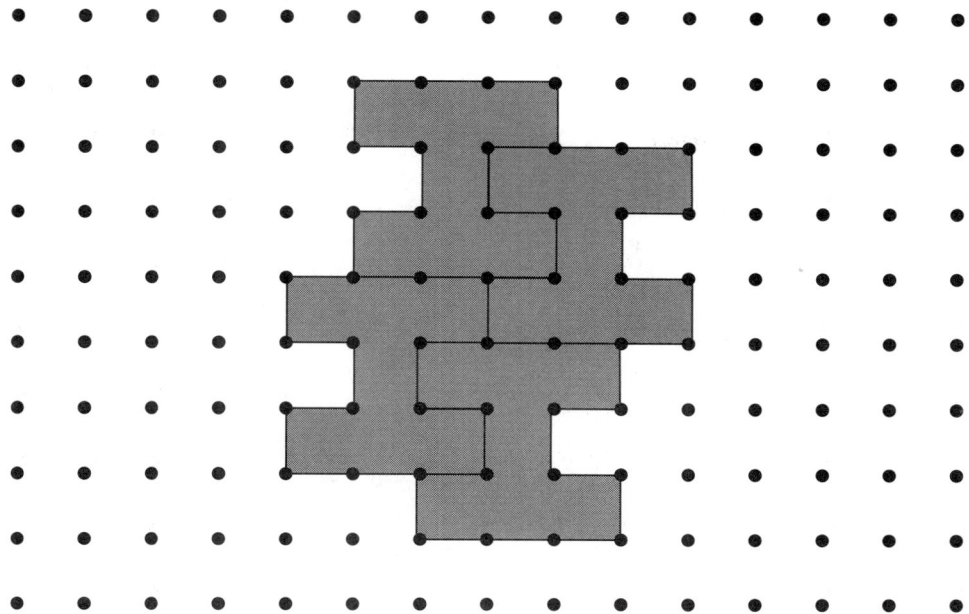

10.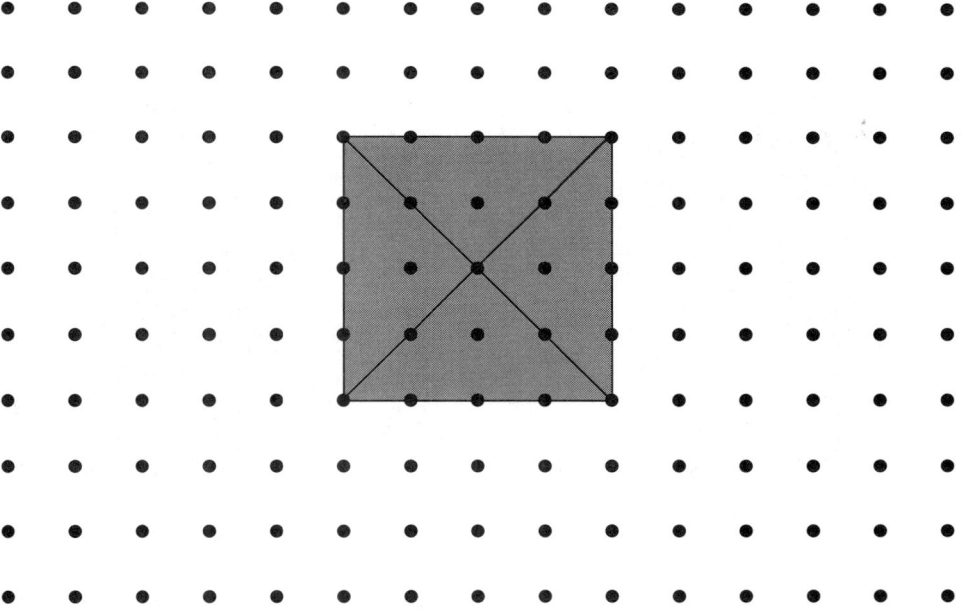

Complete each tessellation by adding 5 more unit shapes to it.

11.

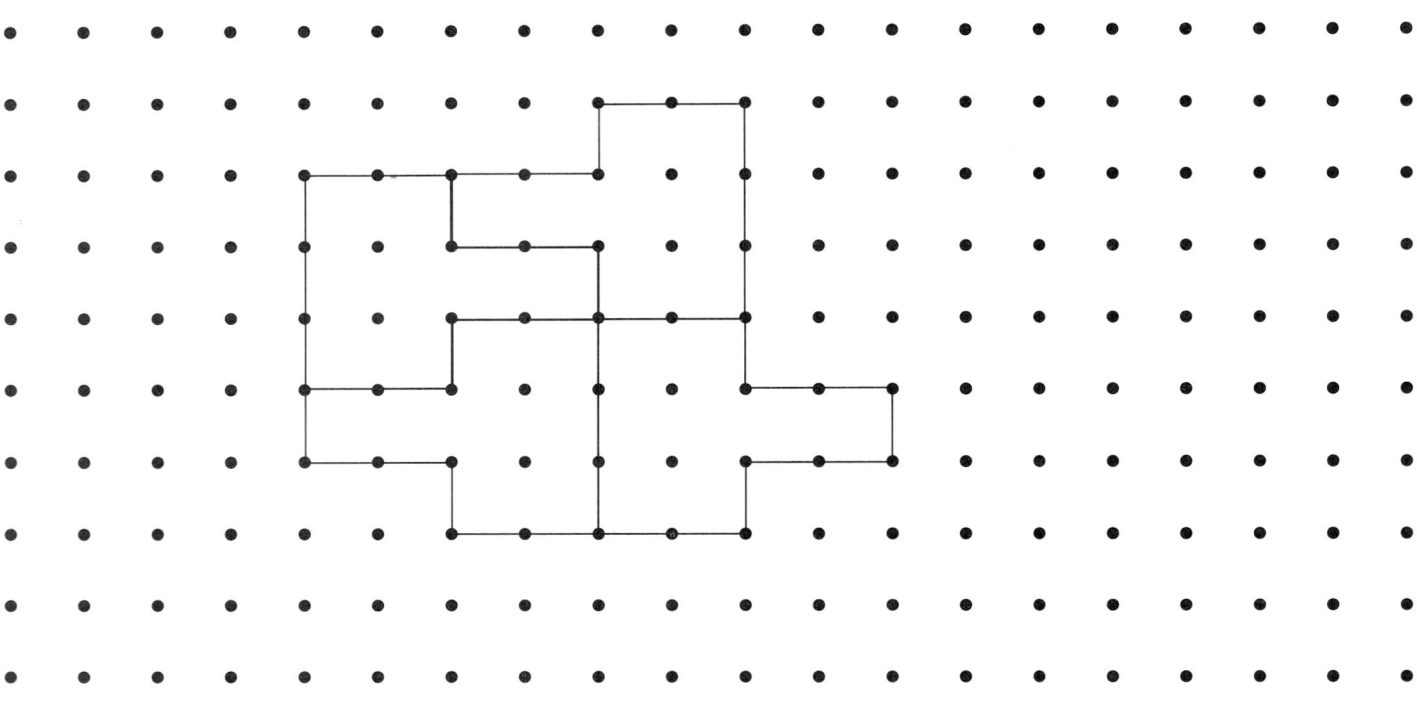

12.

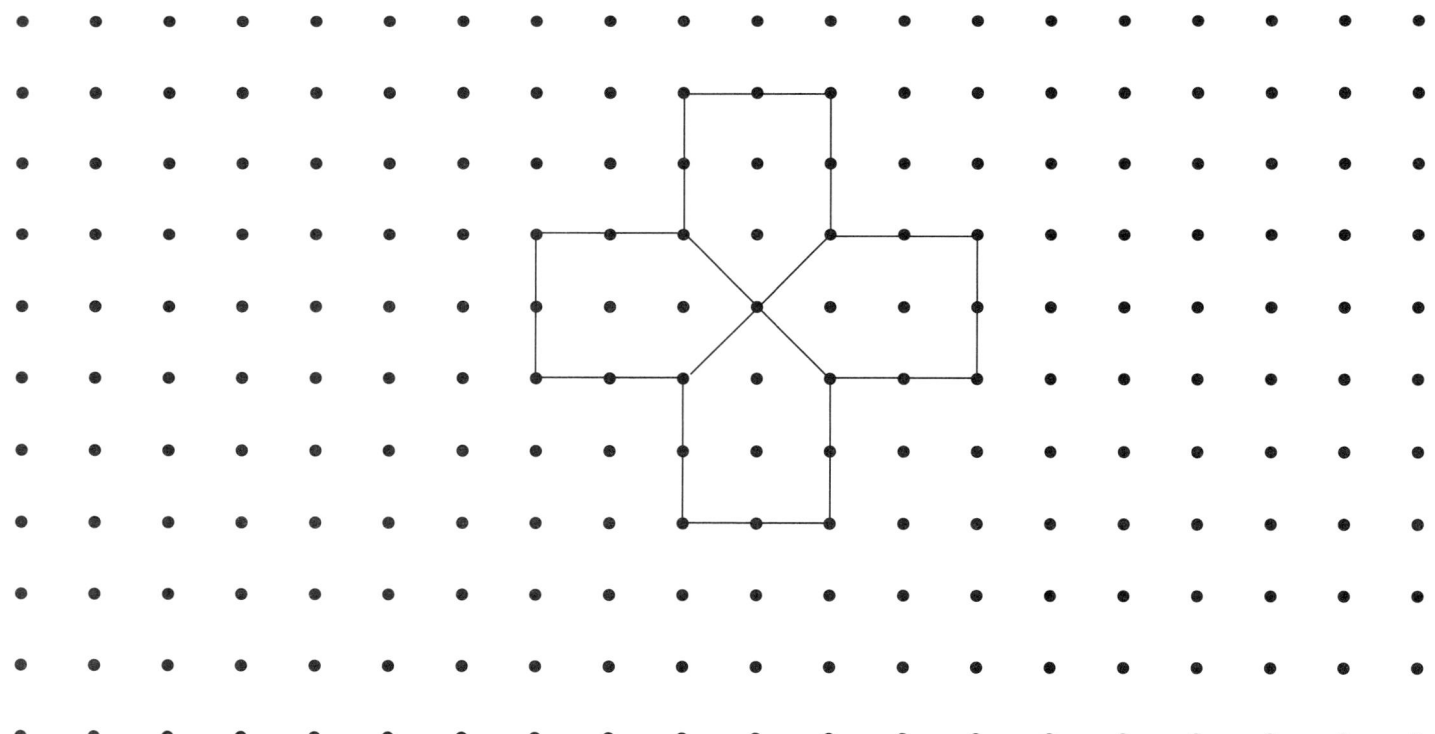

13.

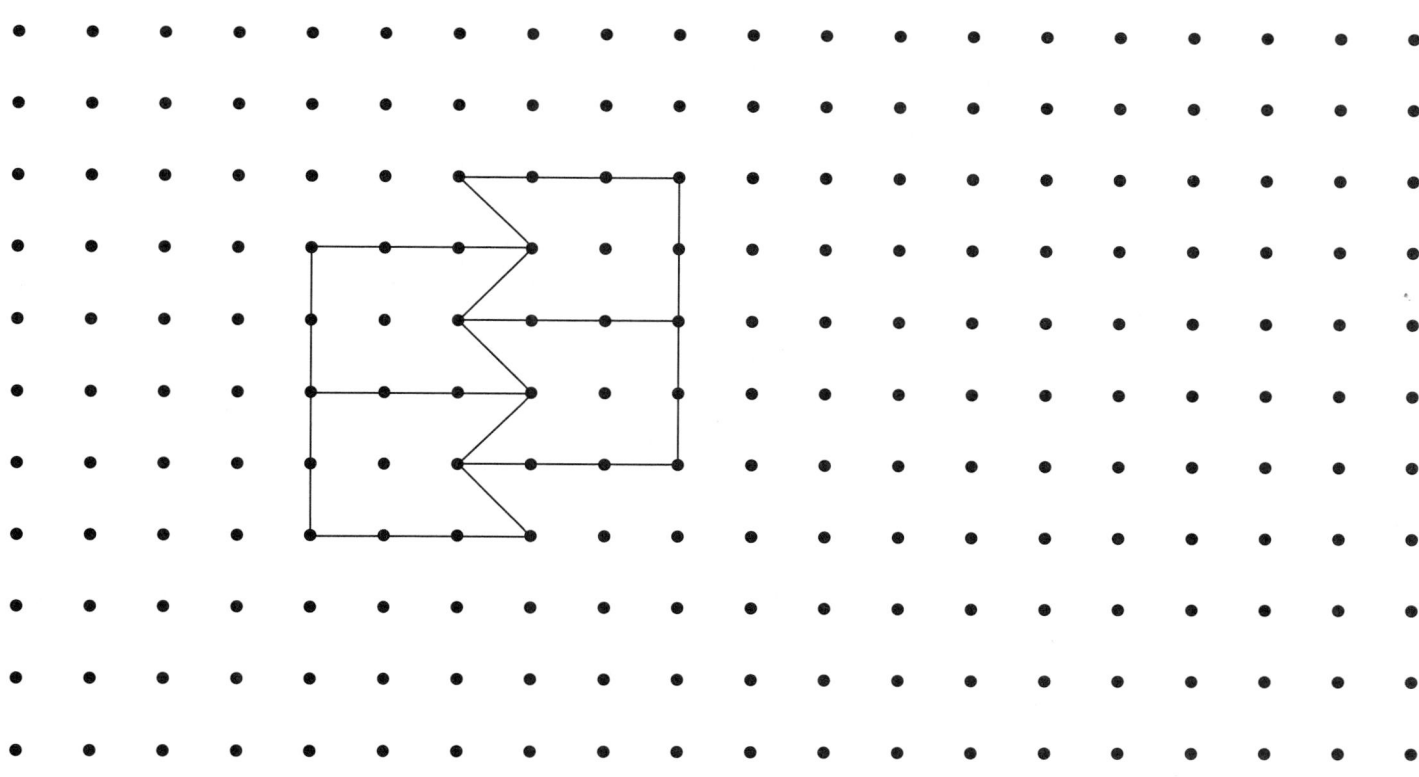

14.

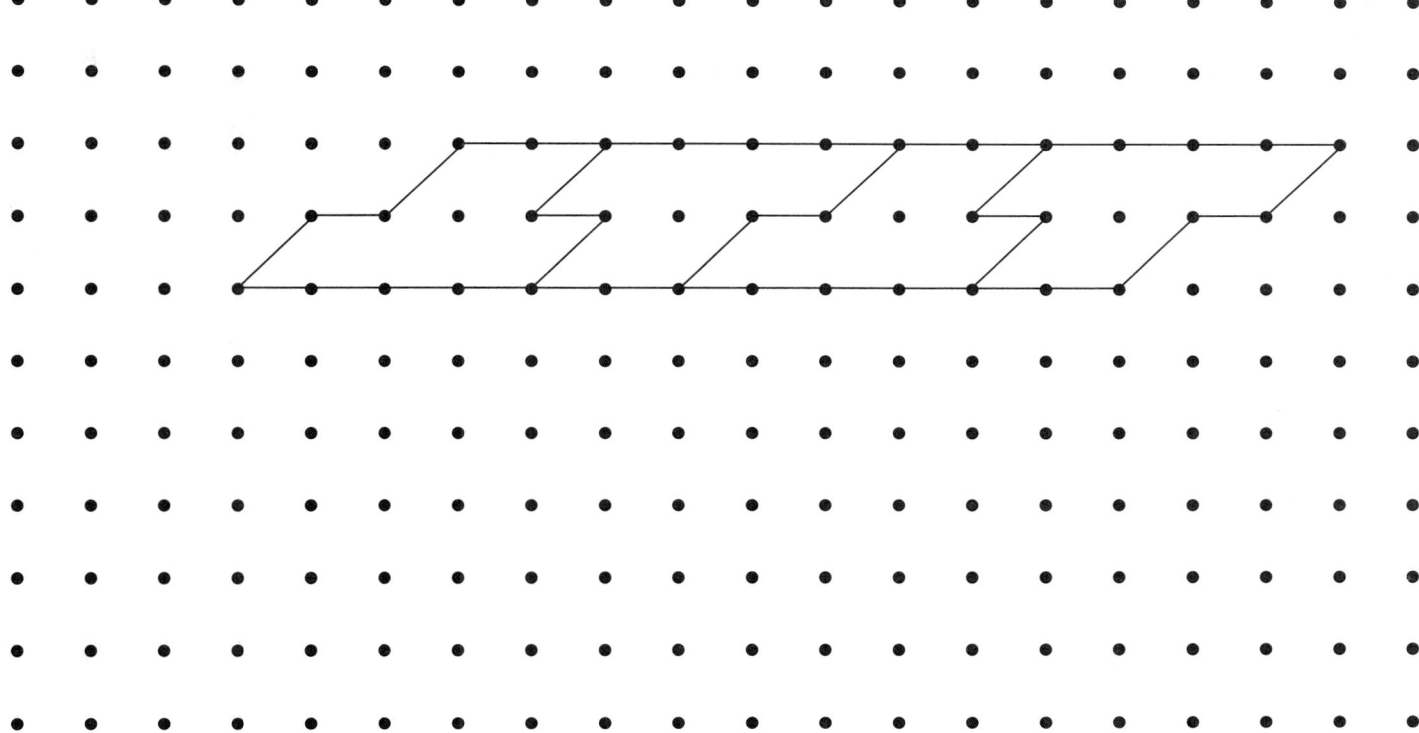

Singapore Math Practice Level 4B

15.

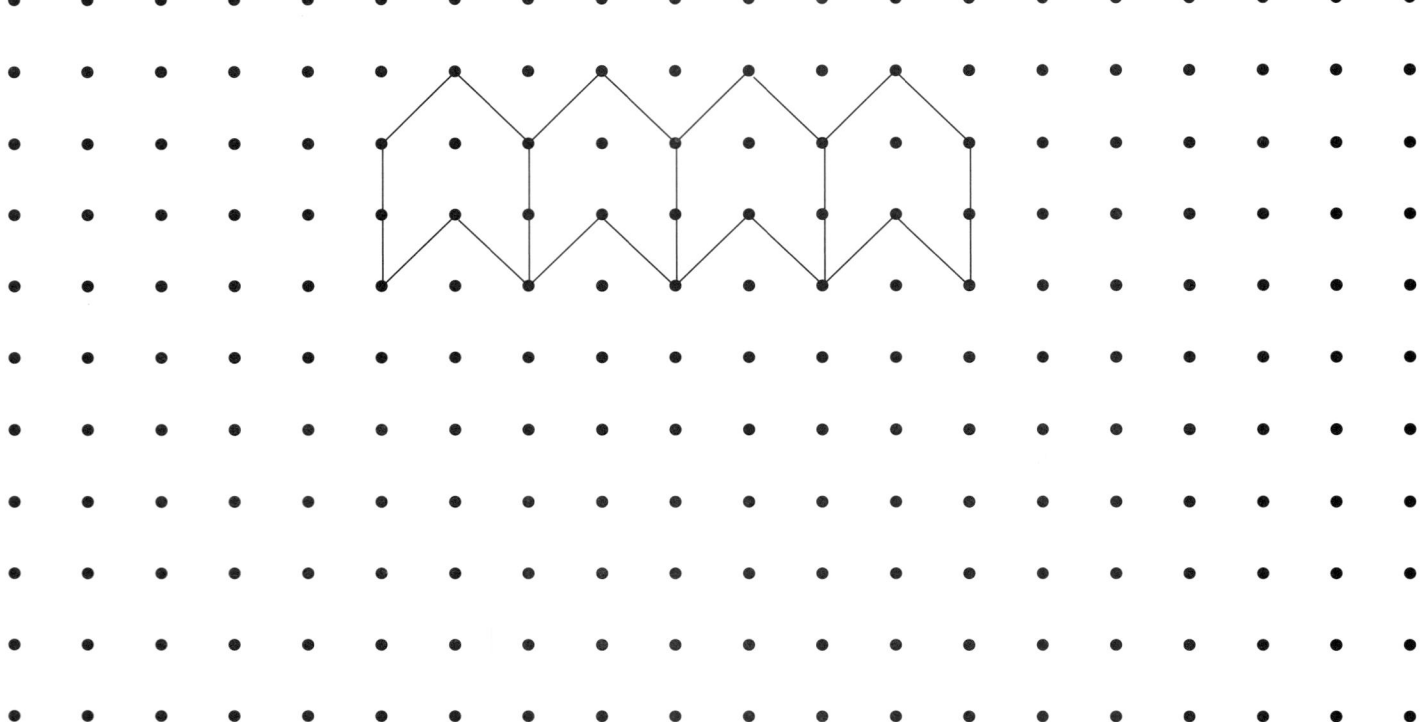

Draw the following shapes in 2 different tessellations. Add at least 5 more unit shapes.

16. (a)

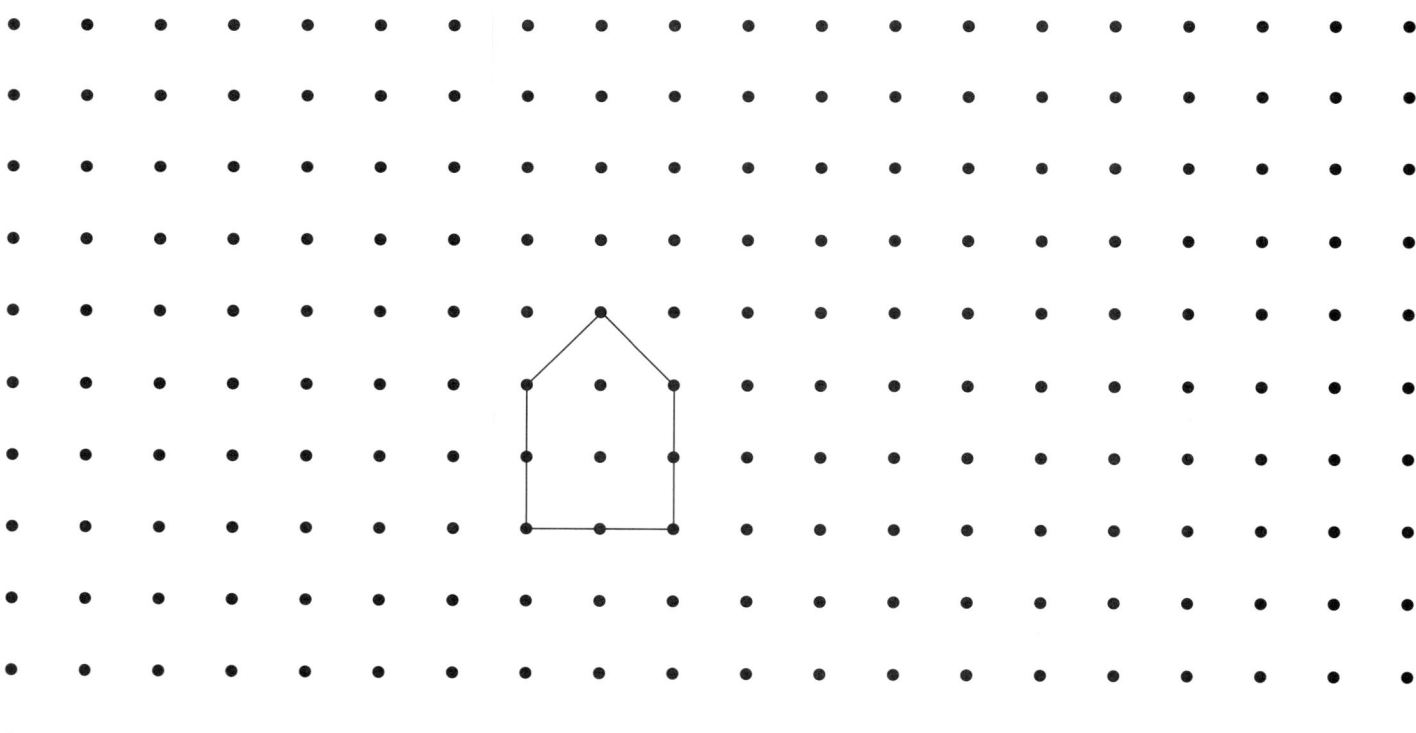

(b)

17. (a)

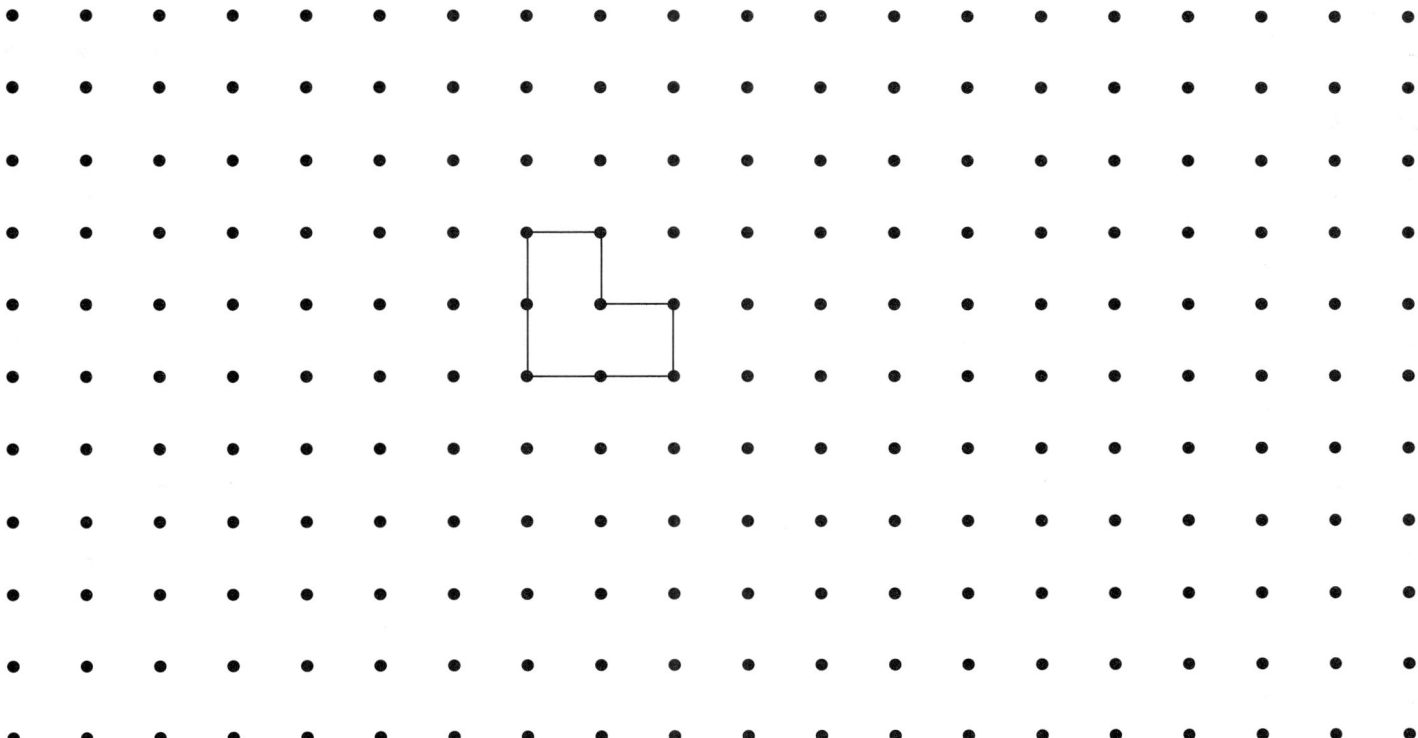

(b)

REVIEW 3

Choose the correct answer. Write its number in the parentheses.

1. Which of the following figures is symmetrical?

   (1) 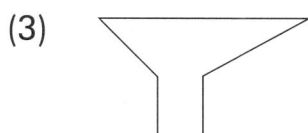   (3)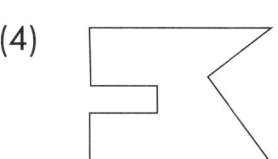

   (2) 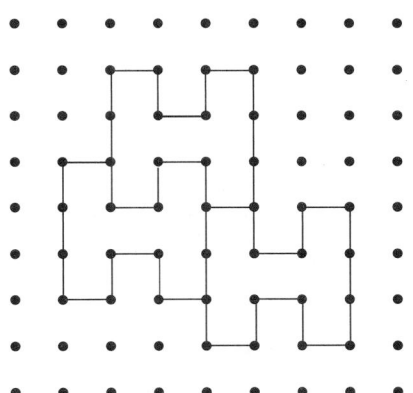   (4)

   (   )

2.

   Which of the following shows the correct unit shape in the tessellation?

   (1) 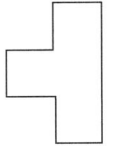   (3)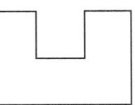

   (2) 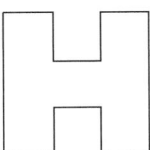   (4)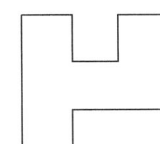

   (   )

3. Which of the following figures are symmetrical?

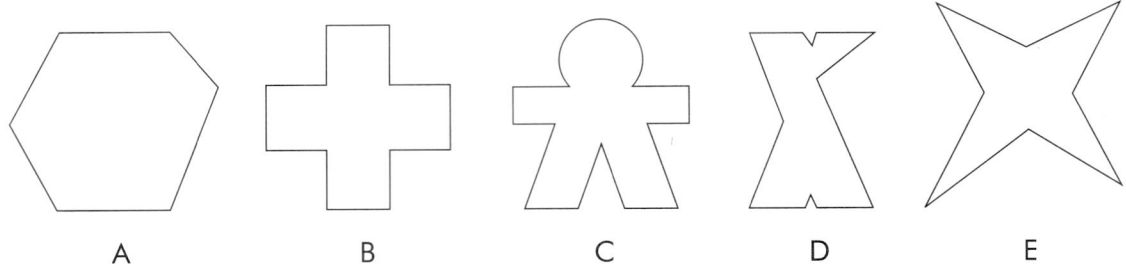

(1) A and C   (3) B and C
(2) A and D   (4) B and E   ( )

4. Which of the following shapes cannot be tessellated?

(1) 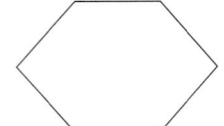   (3)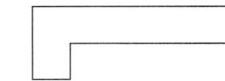

(2) 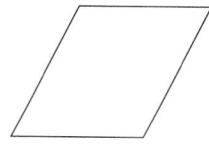   (4)

( )

5. How many more squares must be shaded to make the figure below symmetrical? (2 right-angled triangles make up 1 square.)

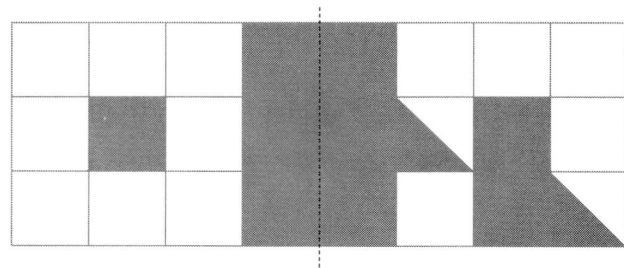

(1) 1   (3) 3
(2) 2   (4) 4   ( )

6. Which of the following shows the correct line of symmetry?

   (1)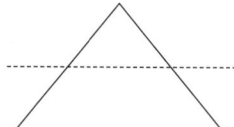

   (2)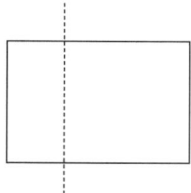

   (3)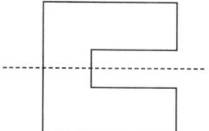

   (4)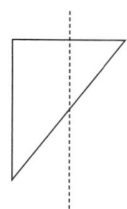

   (   )

7. Which of the following shapes can be tessellated?

   (1)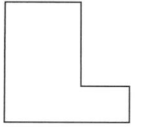

   (2)

   (3)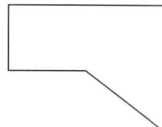

   (4)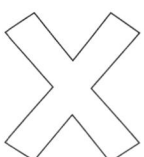

   (   )

Write your answers on the lines.

8. State if the dotted line is a line of symmetry.

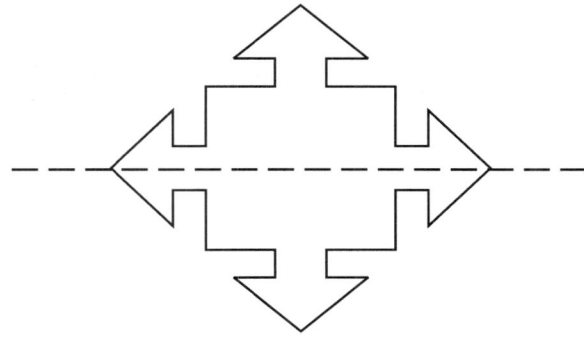

Singapore Math Practice Level 4B

9. The figure below shows half of a symmetrical figure. Line XY is the line of symmetry. Complete the other half of the symmetrical figure.

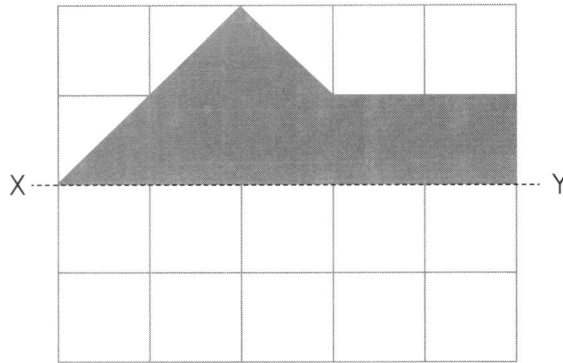

10. Complete the tessellation by adding 5 more unit shapes to it.

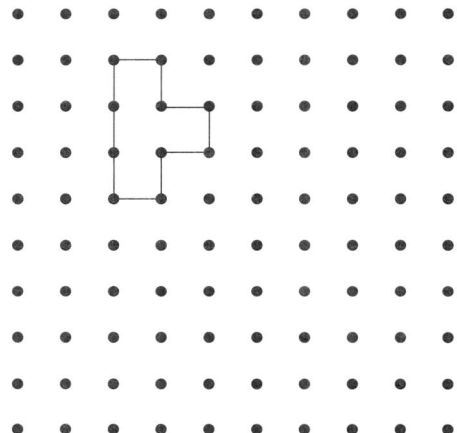

11. Identify the unit shape in the tessellation below by shading it.

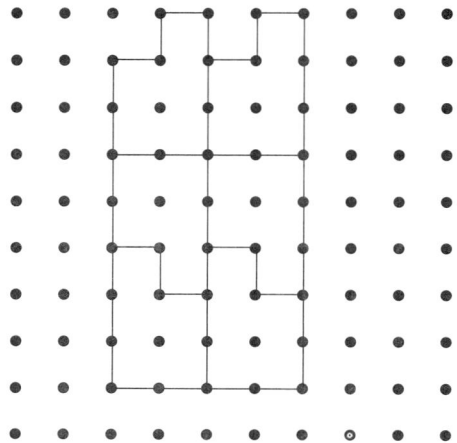

12. Is the figure below symmetrical?

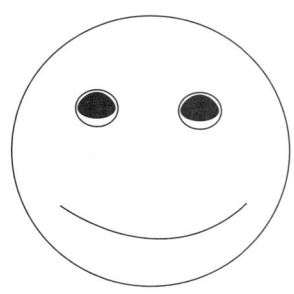

_____

13. Complete the symmetrical figure.

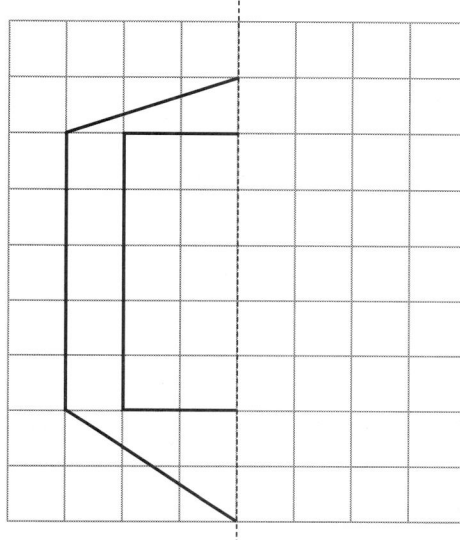

14. Complete the tessellation by adding 5 more unit shapes to it.

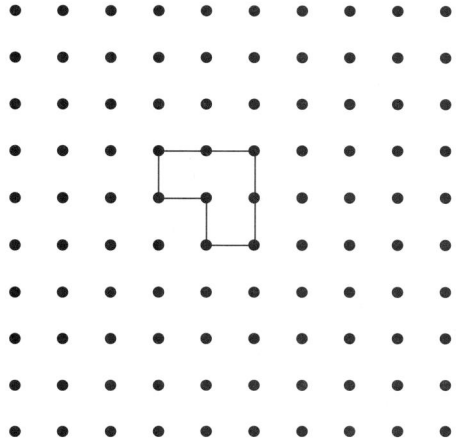

97

Singapore Math Practice Level 4B

15. Complete the symmetrical figure.

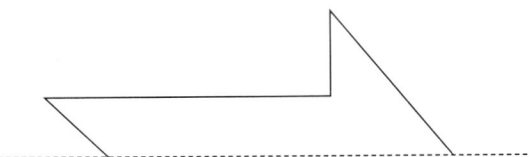

16. State if the dotted line is a line of symmetry.

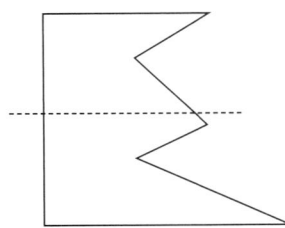

_____

17. Identify the unit shape in the tessellation below by shading it.

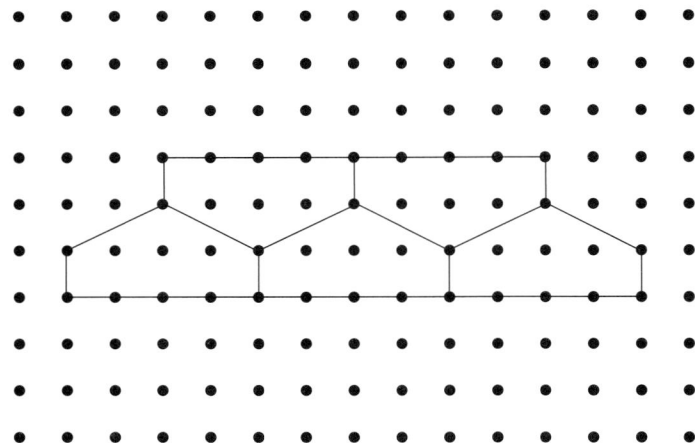

18. Complete the symmetrical figure.

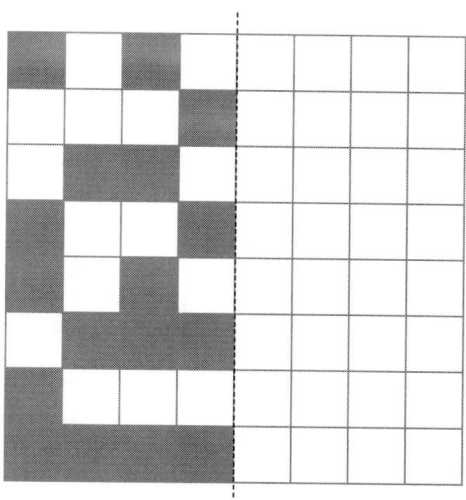

19. State if the letter 'Z' below is symmetrical.

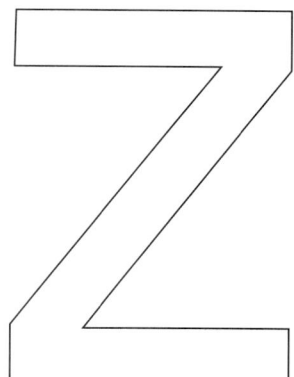

_____

Draw the following shape in 2 different tessellations. Add at least 5 more unit shapes.

20.

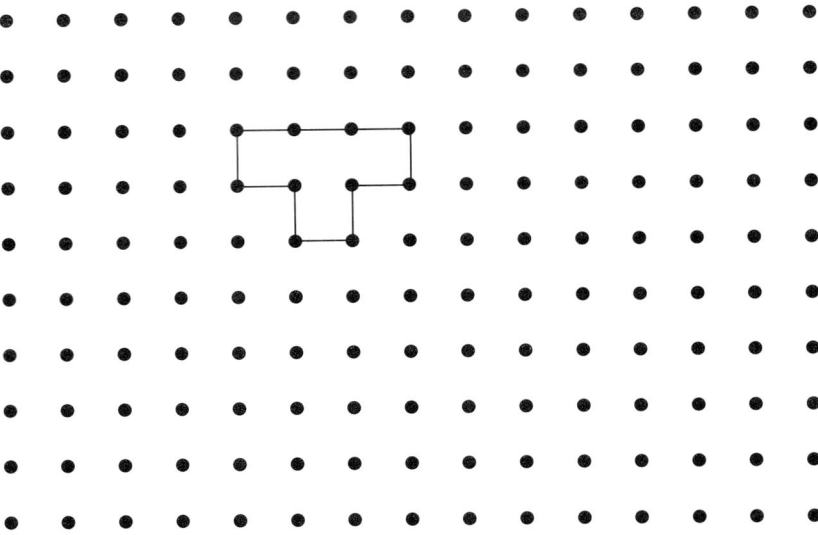

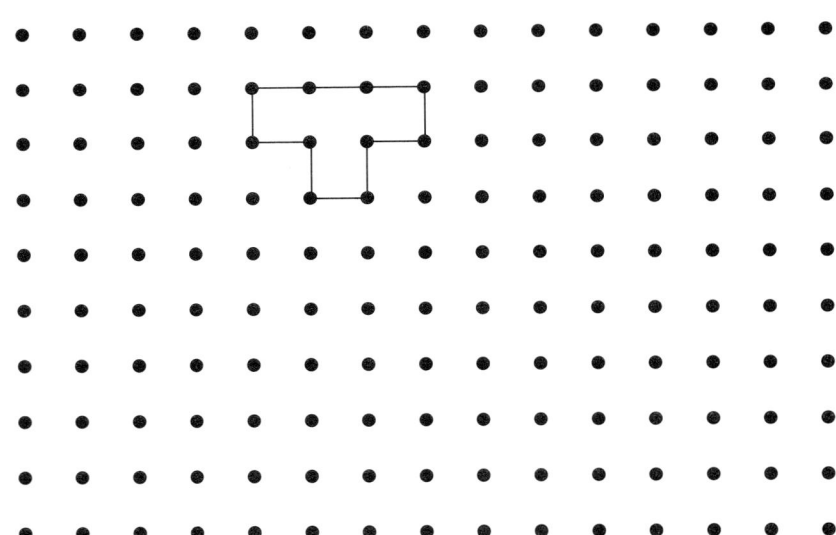

FINAL REVIEW

Choose the correct answer. Write its number in the parentheses.

1. The sum of 28.16 and 5.09 is _____.
   - (1) 32.25
   - (2) 33.16
   - (3) 33.25
   - (4) 34.06   (   )

2. The length of a rope is 5 m when rounded to the nearest meter. Which of the following is the original length of the rope?
   - (1) 4 m 40 cm
   - (2) 4 m 60 cm
   - (3) 5 m 50 cm
   - (4) 5 m 60 cm   (   )

3. Johnny looked at the clock when he was washing his hands. The second hand moved from 3 to 8. He then stopped washing his hands. How long did he wash his hands?
   - (1) 5 sec.
   - (2) 15 sec.
   - (3) 25 sec.
   - (4) 35 sec.   (   )

4. Which of the following numbers is symmetrical?
   - (1) 3
   - (2) 4
   - (3) 5
   - (4) 6   (   )

5. $8.604 = 8 + 0.6 +$ _____
   - (1) 4
   - (2) 0.4
   - (3) 0.04
   - (4) 0.004   (   )

6. Write the time one seventeen and forty-two seconds in the morning.
   - (1) 0117:42
   - (2) 1:17:42 A.M.
   - (3) 1.17:42 A.M.
   - (4) 01:17.42   (   )

Singapore Math Practice Level 4B

7. Write 4 tens, 15 tenths, and 3 hundredths in numerals.
   - (1) 4.153
   - (2) 40.153
   - (3) 40.18
   - (4) 41.53

   ( )

8. $21.04 = 21 + \dfrac{4}{\square}$. What should be the correct answer in the box?
   - (1) 1
   - (2) 10
   - (3) 100
   - (4) 1000

   ( )

9. The perimeter of a square is 64 in. Find its length.
   - (1) 8 in.
   - (2) 16 in.
   - (3) 18 in.
   - (4) 32 in.

   ( )

10. Express 405 hundredths as a decimal.
    - (1) 0.405
    - (2) 4.05
    - (3) 40.5
    - (4) 400.5

    ( )

11. The product of 93.28 and 8 is _____.
    - (1) 11.66
    - (2) 85.28
    - (3) 101.28
    - (4) 746.24

    ( )

12. Which of the following figures below is **not** symmetrical?
    - (1)
    - (2)
    - (3)
    - (4)

    ( )

13. Fiona watched a cartoon at 7:30 P.M. If the cartoon ended at 9:10 P.M., how long was the cartoon?

    (1) 1 hr. 20 min.
    (2) 1 hr. 40 min.
    (3) 2 hr. 10 min.
    (4) 2 hr. 20 min.   (   )

14. Lisa bought 5.4 kg of sugar. She packed the sugar equally into 4 bags. What was the mass of each bag of sugar?

    (1) 1.26 kg
    (2) 1.35 kg
    (3) 9.4 kg
    (4) 21.6 kg   (   )

15. Mrs. Volkmer sold 100 cookies. She sold them at $2.05 for 10 cookies. How much money did she collect from selling the cookies?

    (1) $20.50
    (2) $25
    (3) $200.50
    (4) $205   (   )

16. Ben took 18.35 sec. to complete a 100-yard race. Daniel finished the race 3.2 sec. faster than Ben. How long did Daniel take to finish the race?

    (1) 15.15 sec.
    (2) 15.33 sec.
    (3) 18.07 sec.
    (4) 21.55 sec.   (   )

17. The perimeter of a square is 20 ft. Find its area.

    (1) 16 ft.^{2}
    (2) 25 ft.^{2}
    (3) 80 ft.^{2}
    (4) 400 ft.^{2} (   )

18. The figure, not drawn to scale, is made up of 5 similar squares. Find its perimeter.

    (1) 16 cm
    (2) 32 cm
    (3) 48 cm
    (4) 80 cm

                                                            (   )

Singapore Math Practice Level 4B

19. Which of the following decimals is 10 when rounding to the nearest whole number?

    (1) 9.09 (3) 10.5
    (2) 9.9   (4) 10.9   ( )

20. In 805.139, which digit is in the thousandths place?

    (1) 3   (3) 8
    (2) 5   (4) 9   ( )

Write your answers on the lines.

21. The shaded parts represent the decimal. Write down the correct decimal.

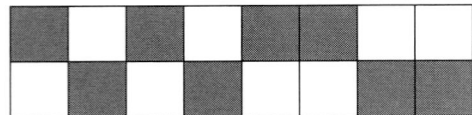

_____

22. Tomas reached the library at 9:15 A.M. He stayed there for 3 hr. 55 min. At what time did he leave the library?

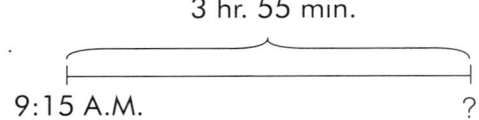

_____

23. Express $\frac{4}{5}$ as a decimal.   _____

24. Shade 0.25 of the figure below.

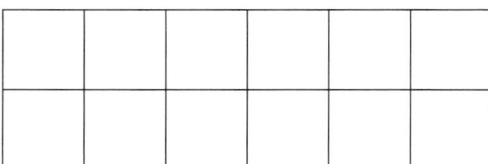

25. State if the shape below is symmetrical.

_____

26. Identify the unit shape in the tessellation below by shading it.

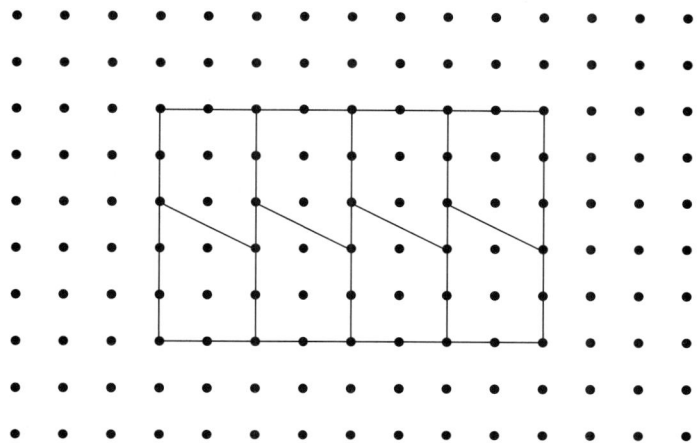

27. Arrange the decimals in descending order.

   7.8   0.78   7.08

_____

28. The figure below is made up of three rectangles. Find its area.

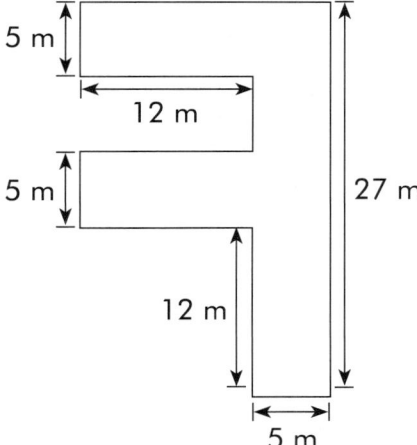

_____

Singapore Math Practice Level 4B

29. Complete the symmetrical figure.

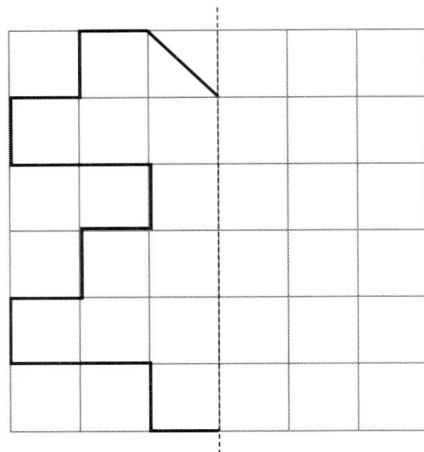

30. Estimate the value of 41.8 ÷ 6.

_____

31. A clock shows 4:40 P.M. If the clock is 45 minutes slow, write the correct time.

_____

32. The figure is made up of 5 squares. Find its area.

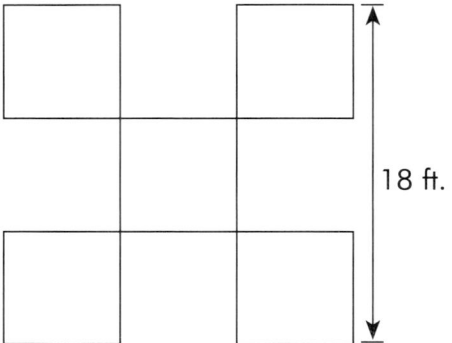

18 ft.

_____

33. Complete the symmetrical pattern below using Line AB as the line of symmetry.

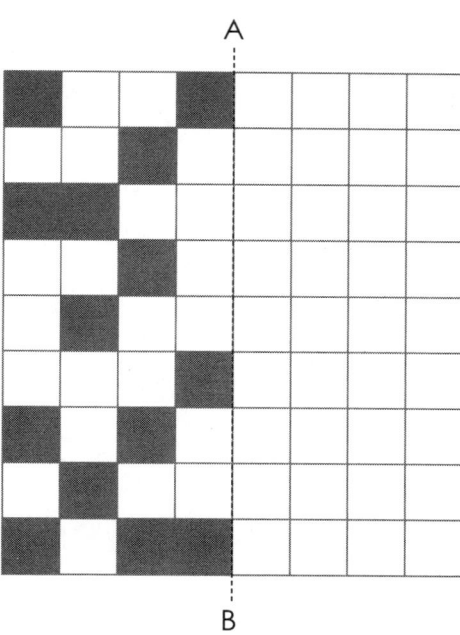

34. Rudy poured 9 gallons of syrup into 5 bottles equally. How much syrup was there in each bottle?

_____

35. Complete the tessellation below by adding 5 more unit shapes.

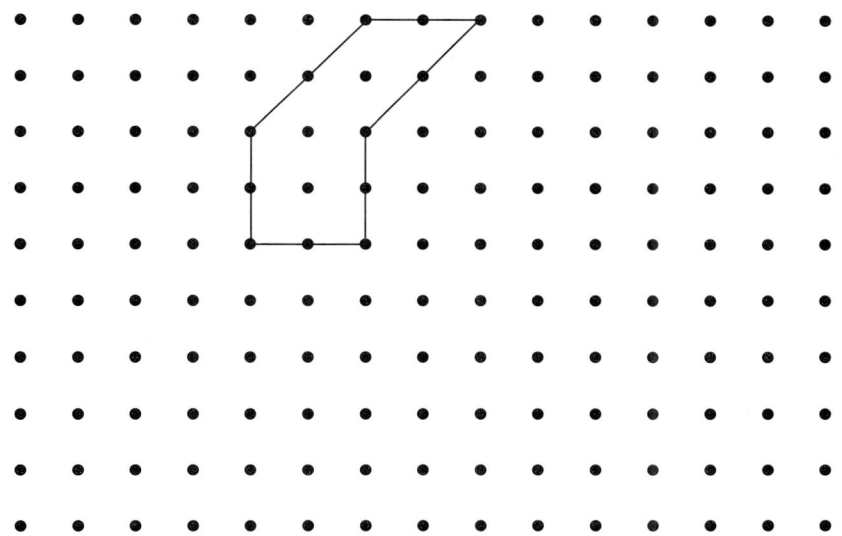

Singapore Math Practice Level 4B

36. A garden has an area of 96 yd.². Its width is 6 yd. Find its perimeter.

    _____

37. In 127.04, the digit 0 is in the _____ place.   _____

38. Fill in each box with the correct decimal.

    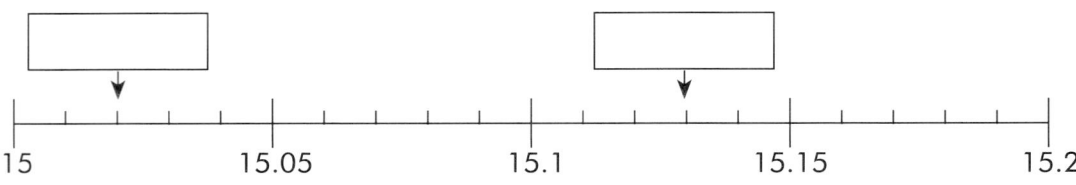

39.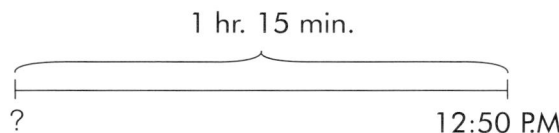

    Cara got off the bus at 12:50 P.M. If the trip took 1 hr. 15 min., at what time did she board the bus?

    _____

40. State if the unit shape below can be tessellated.

    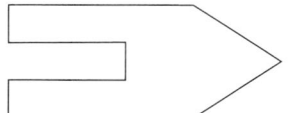

    _____

108

Singapore Math Practice Level 4B

Solve the following story problems. Show your work in the space below.

41. Mrs. Brown bought 13 lb. of meat. Each pound of meat cost $9.65. She gave the cashier $150. How much change did she receive?

42. A bus left Townsville at 7:05 P.M. It traveled for 3 hr. 40 min. and stopped for a rest. The bus continued the journey and reached Garden Town at 3:30 A.M. If the second part of the journey was 4 hr. 10 min., how long did it stop for a rest?

Singapore Math Practice Level 4B

43. To make a bottle of fruit punch, 0.84 L of orange juice, 0.47 L of ginger ale, and 0.65 L of pineapple juice are needed. How many liters of fruit punch are there in a dozen bottles?

44. Charlene used 1.6 m of ribbon to tie a large present. She used another 95 cm of ribbon to tie a small present. If she had 5 m of ribbon in the beginning, how many meters of ribbon did she have left?

45. A carpet is placed in the middle of a square hall as shown below. What is the total cost of the carpet if it costs $19 per yd.²?

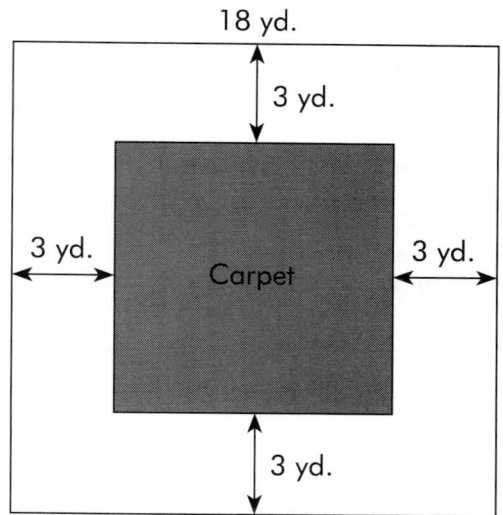

CHALLENGE QUESTIONS

Solve the following problems on another sheet of paper.

1. Study the pattern carefully and draw the correct shape in the given box.

 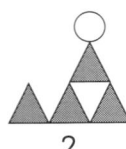 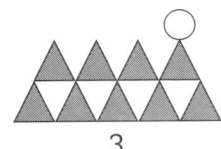 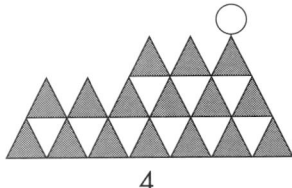 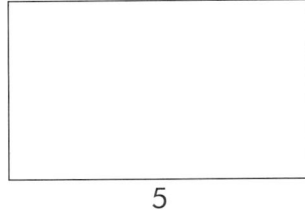

  1   2   3   4   5

2. A group of students were told that they would have their afternoon break when the hour hand and minute hand formed a right angle on the clock. If the minute hand pointed to 12, what was the time of their afternoon break?

3. Two similar television sets and one DVD player cost $919.70.
   One television set and two similar DVD players cost $639.70.
   How much do three television sets cost?

4. The area of the bigger square is 576 in.². The area of the shaded square is 144 in.². Find the length of x.

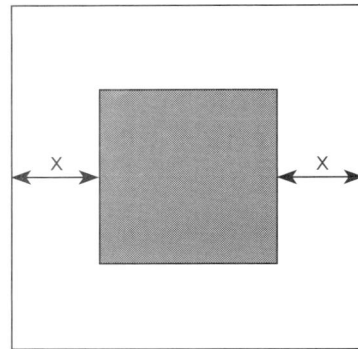

5. Several 3-cm cubes are arranged to form a solid as shown below. Find the total perimeter of all the faces of the solid.

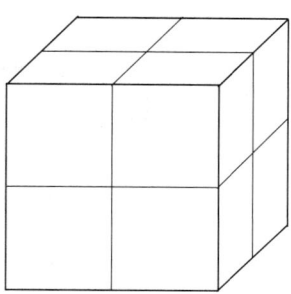

6. Mrs. Munoz sold three times as much lemon tea on Saturday than on Monday. She sold 5 times as much lemon tea on Sunday than on Monday. If Mrs. Munoz sold 2 liters 600 milliliters more of lemon tea on Sunday than on Saturday, how much lemon tea did Mrs. Munoz sell over the weekend?

7. How many 1-in. cubes are needed to make this 3-in. solid?

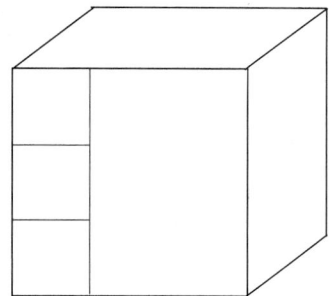

8. Three similar books and two similar dictionaries cost $85.50.
One book and one dictionary cost $37.80.
How much is each book?

Singapore Math Practice Level 4B

9. The length of the bigger square is 64 cm. Find the area of the unshaded square.

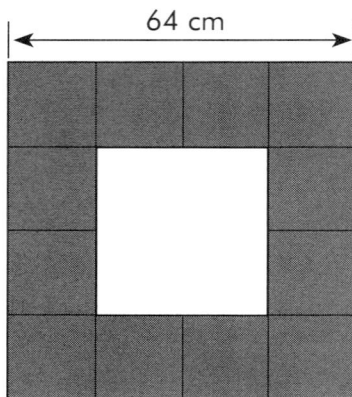

10. Circle the letter(s) that is/are **not** symmetrical.

    A S V M K

11. How many 5-cm cubes are needed to form a solid of 3,125 cm³?

12. Keith took an hour to paint 5 similar chairs. If he worked 8 hours a day, how many days did he use to paint 120 similar chairs?

SOLUTIONS
Singapore Math Practice Level 4B

Unit 9: Decimals (Part 1)

1. $\frac{4}{10}$ = **0.4**
2. $\frac{6}{10}$ = **0.6**
3. $\frac{2}{10}$ = **0.2**
4. $\frac{7}{10}$ = **0.7**
5. $\frac{1}{10}$ = **0.1**
6. $\frac{7}{10}$ = **0.7**
7. $3\frac{2}{10}$ = **3.2**
8. 13 tenths = 1 one 3 tenths
    $4\frac{13}{10} = 5\frac{3}{10}$ = **5.3**
9. 18 tenths = 1 one 8 tenths
    $2\frac{18}{10} = 3\frac{8}{10}$ = **3.8**
10. 24 tenths = 2 ones 4 tenths
    $9\frac{24}{10} = 11\frac{4}{10}$ = **11.4**
11. **9**
    $0.9 = \frac{9}{10}$ = 9 tenths
12. **36**
    $3.6 = 3\frac{6}{10}$ = 3 ones 6 tenths = 36 tenths
13. **784**
    $78.4 = 78\frac{4}{10}$ = 78 ones 4 tenths = 784 tenths
14. **183**
    $18.3 = 18\frac{3}{10}$ = 18 ones 3 tenths = 183 tenths
15. **215**
    $21.5 = 21\frac{5}{10}$ = 21 ones 5 tenths = 215 tenths
16. **1.4**, **2.9**
    Each marking on the number line is 0.1.
17. **2.7**, **4.8**
    Each marking on the number line is 0.1.
18. **6.9**, **7.6**
    Each marking on the number line is 0.1.
19. **9**
20. **4**
21. **3**
22. **6**
23. **8**
24. (a) **1**
    (b) **tenths**
    (c) **90**
    (d) **1**
25. (a) **5**
    (b) **tenths**
    (c) **7**
    (d) **5 tens/50**
26. $0.26 = \frac{26}{100}$
    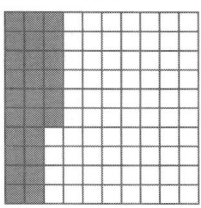
27. $0.74 = \frac{74}{100}$
    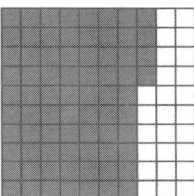
28. $0.03 = \frac{3}{100}$
    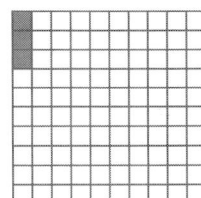
29. $0.62 = \frac{62}{100}$
    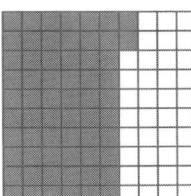
30. $0.45 = \frac{45}{100}$
    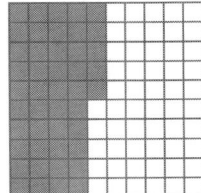

31. $\frac{8}{100} = $ **0.08**
32. $\frac{16}{100} = $ **0.16**
33. $\frac{32}{100} = $ **0.32**
34. $\frac{188}{100} = 1 + \frac{88}{100} = $ **1.88**
35. $\frac{311}{100} = 3 + \frac{11}{100} = $ **3.11**
36. **543**
    $5.43 = 5\frac{43}{100} = $ 5 ones 43 hundredths
    $= $ 543 hundredths
37. **8,195**
    $81.95 = 81\frac{95}{100} = $ 81 ones 95 hundredths
    $= $ 8,195 hundredths
38. **6,072**
    $60.72 = 60\frac{72}{100} = $ 60 ones 72 hundredths
    $= $ 6,072 hundredths
39. **3,854**
    $38.54 = 38\frac{54}{100} = $ 38 ones 54 hundredths
    $= $ 3,854 hundredths
40. **9,045**
    $90.45 = 90\frac{45}{100} = $ 90 ones 45 hundredths
    $= $ 9,045 hundredths
41. **0.12, 0.25**
    Each marking on the number line is 0.01.
42. **0.57, 0.66**
    Each marking on the number line is 0.01.
43. **0.86, 0.95**
    Each marking on the number line is 0.01.
44. **2, 0, 4, 5**
45. **7, 1, 3, 8**
46. **9, 4, 2, 8**
47. **6, 4, 1, 3**
48. **5, 2, 5, 6**
49. (a) **0**
    (b) **tens**
    (c) **0.2/2 tenths**
    (d) **0.04**
    (e) **70**
50. (a) **1**
    (b) **tens**
    (c) **3/3 ones**
    (d) **0.08**
    (e) **0.1**
51. $\frac{4}{1,000} = $ **0.004**
52. $\frac{15}{1,000} = $ **0.015**
53. $\frac{291}{1,000} = $ **0.291**
54. $\frac{718}{1,000} = $ **0.718**
55. $\frac{1,414}{1,000} = $ **1.414**
56. $\frac{2,086}{1,000} = $ **2.086**

57. **28,404**
    $28.404 = 28\frac{404}{1,000} = $ 28 ones 404 thousandths
    $= $ 28,404 thousandths
58. **40,687**
    $40.687 = 40\frac{687}{1,000} = $ 40 ones 687 thousandths
    $= $ 40,687 thousandths
59. **53,936**
    $53.936 = 53\frac{936}{1,000} = $ 53 ones 936 thousandths
    $= $ 53,936 thousandths
60. **2,308**
    $2.308 = 2\frac{308}{1,000} = $ 2 ones 308 thousandths
    $= $ 2,308 thousandths
61. **66,799**
    $66.799 = 66\frac{799}{1,000} = $ 66 ones 799 thousandths
    $= $ 66,799 thousandths
62. **5.008, 5.017**
    Each marking on the number line is 0.001.
63. **9.001, 9.011**
    Each marking on the number line is 0.001.
64. **10.007, 10.014**
    Each marking on the number line is 0.001.
65. **2, 0, 0, 4, 5**
66. **5, 8, 2, 9, 7**
67. **7, 2, 3, 9, 3**
68. **3, 6, 8, 1, 6**
69. **8, 4, 0, 3, 5**
70. (a) **7**
    (b) **tenths**
    (c) **0.08/8 hundredths**
    (d) **0.007**
    (e) **4**
71. (a) **0**
    (b) **thousandths**
    (c) **0.9/9 tenths**
    (d) **10**
    (e) **0.06**
72. **14.4**
    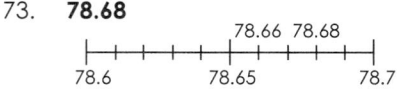
73. **78.68**
    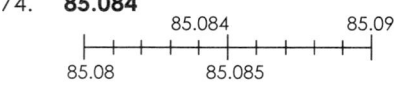
74. **85.084**
    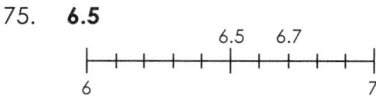
75. **6.5**
76. **57.02**
77.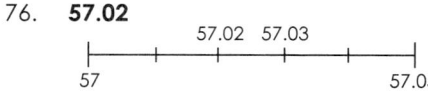
    3.8, 4.7, 5.6, **6.5**, **7.4**

78. 15.34, 15.39, 15.44, **15.49**, **15.54** (+ 0.05 each)
79. 45.06, 45.09, 45.12, **45.15**, **45.18** (+ 0.03 each)
80. 10.088, 10.089, 10.09, **10.091**, **10.092** (+ 0.001 each)
81. 82.309, 82.314, 82.319, **82.324**, **82.329** (+ 0.005 each)
82. **1.8**
    Since all have the same ones, compare the tenths. 8 tenths is the largest.
83. **3.65**
    $3\frac{605}{1,000} = 3.605$ $\frac{365}{1,000} = 0.365$
    Compare the ones first. Then compare the tenths and hundredths. 3.65 is the largest.
84. **2.91**
    $2\frac{901}{1,000} = 2.901$ $2\frac{29}{100} = 2.09$
    Compare the ones first. Next, compare the tenths and hundredths. Hence, 2.91 is the largest.
85. **7.012**
    Since all have the same ones, compare the tenths. Next, compare the hundredths. 0 hundredths is the smallest.
86. **$\frac{8,059}{1,000}$**
    $8\frac{95}{100} = 8.95$ $\frac{8,059}{1,000} = 8.059$
    Since all have the same ones, compare the tenths. Next, compare the hundredths. 5 hundredths is the smallest.
87. **$\frac{399}{1,000}$**
    $3\frac{909}{1,000} = 3.909$ $3\frac{99}{1,000} = 3.099$ $\frac{399}{1,000} = 0.399$
    Compare the ones first. 0 ones is the smallest.
88. **5.28, 5.028, 2.058**
89. **4.502, 4.25, 4.025**
90. **9.01, 1.09, 0.19**
91. **198.003, 198.03, 198.3**
92. **27.329, 273.29, 2,732.9**
93. **6.017, 6.107, 6.17**
94. 1.04 ≈ **1**
95. 2.55 ≈ **3**
96. 15.82 ≈ **16**
97. 0.95 ≈ **1**
98. 7.74 ≈ **8**
99. 1.68 ≈ **1.7**
100. 33.38 ≈ **33.4**
101. 2.91 ≈ **2.9**
102. 14.74 ≈ **14.7**
103. 6.472 ≈ **6.5**
104. 89.943 ≈ **89.9**
105. 10.963 ≈ **10.96**
106. 59.095 ≈ **59.10**
107. 7.007 ≈ **7.01**
108. 0.671 ≈ **0.67**
109. 2.386 ≈ **2.39**
110. 15.709 ≈ **15.71**
111. $\frac{4}{10} = $ **0.4**
112. $\frac{11}{10} = \frac{10}{10} + \frac{1}{10} = 1 + 0.1 = $ **1.1**
113. $5\frac{8}{10} = 5 + \frac{8}{10} = 5 + 0.8 = $ **5.8**
114. $9\frac{4 \times 2}{5 \times 2} = 9\frac{8}{10} = $ **9.8**
115. $\frac{1}{100} = $ **0.01**
116. $\frac{28}{100} = $ **0.28**
117. $1\frac{77}{100} = $ **1.77**
118. $4\frac{18 \times 4}{25 \times 4} = 4\frac{72}{100} = $ **4.72**
119. $\frac{462}{1,000} = $ **0.462**
120. $\frac{9}{1,000} = $ **0.009**
121. $5\frac{16}{1,000} = $ **5.016**
122. $45\frac{45 \times 2}{50 \times 2} = 45\frac{90}{100} = $ **45.9**
123. $6.2 = \frac{62}{10} = 6\frac{2}{10} = 6\frac{1}{5}$
124. $49.4 = \frac{494}{10} = 49\frac{4}{10} = $ **$49\frac{2}{5}$**
125. $7.08 = \frac{708}{100} = 7\frac{8}{100} = $ **$7\frac{2}{25}$**
126. $51.25 = \frac{5,125}{100} = 51\frac{25}{100} = $ **$51\frac{1}{4}$**
127. $1.008 = \frac{1,008}{1,000} = 1\frac{8}{1,000} = $ **$1\frac{1}{125}$**
128. $25.42 = \frac{2,542}{100} = 25\frac{42}{100} = $ **$25\frac{21}{50}$**

Unit 10: Decimals (Part 2)

1.   0.1
   + 0.3

     0.4

2.   6.2
   + 1.3

     7.5

3.   9.08
   + 5.57

    14.65

4.   5.14
   + 13.63

    18.77

5.   56.01
   + 72.96

    128.97

6. $\overset{11}{39.78}$
    $+44.05$
    ―――――
    83.83

7. 0.5
    -0.2
    ―――
    0.3

8. 9.7
    -5.4
    ―――
    4.3

9. $4.\overset{511}{\cancel{6}\cancel{1}}$
    -2.39
    ―――――
    2.22

10. $\overset{111}{\cancel{2}\cancel{1}.75}$
    -8.03
    ―――――
    13.72

11. $9\overset{613}{\cancel{7}.\cancel{3}6}$
    -50.72
    ―――――
    46.64

12. $\overset{7914}{\cancel{8}\cancel{0}.\cancel{4}9}$
    -31.67
    ―――――
    48.82

13. 5.1
    $\times2$
    ―――――
    10.2

14. $\overset{2}{0}.4$
    $\times5$
    ―――――
    2.0

15. $\overset{3}{3}.8$
    $\times4$
    ―――――
    15.2

16. $\overset{1}{2}.3$
    $\times6$
    ―――――
    13.8

17. $8.\overset{14}{1}7$
    $\times7$
    ―――――
    57.19

18. $\overset{11}{3}.45$
    $\times3$
    ―――――
    10.35

19. $0.\overset{77}{7}8$
    $\times9$
    ―――――
    7.02

20. $\overset{113}{12.36}$
    $\times5$
    ―――――
    61.80

21. 50.12
    $\times2$
    ―――――
    100.24

22. $\overset{33}{21.55}$
    $\times6$
    ―――――
    129.30

23. 2.6
    $3\overline{)7.8}$
    6
    ―――
    18
    18
    ―――
    0

24. 1.05
    $5\overline{)5.25}$
    5
    ―――
    2
    0
    ―――
    25
    25
    ―――
    0

25. 2.445
    $2\overline{)4.890}$
    4
    ―――
    8
    8
    ―――
    9
    8
    ―――
    10
    10
    ―――
    0

26. 4.1
    $4\overline{)16.4}$
    16.4
    ―――
    4
    4
    ―――
    0

27. 3.05
    $9\overline{)27.45}$
    27
    ―――
    4
    0
    ―――
    45
    45
    ―――
    0

28. 10.85
    $4\overline{)43.40}$
    4
    ―――
    3
    0
    ―――
    34
    32
    ―――
    20
    20
    ―――
    0

29. 90.3
    $9\overline{)812.7}$
    81
    ―――
    2
    0
    ―――
    27
    27
    ―――
    0

30.
```
      6 7 . 0 2 5
   6 ) 4 0 2 . 1 5
       3 6
       ─────
         4 2
         4 2
         ─────
            1
            0
            ─────
            1 5
            1 2
            ─────
              3 0
              3 0
              ─────
                0
```

31.
```
      3 . 6
   3 ) 1 8
       1 5
       ───
         3 0
         3 0
         ───
            0
```

32.
```
      1 . 2 5
   8 ) 1 0 . 0 0
       8
       ─────
       2 0
       1 6
       ─────
         4 0
         4 0
         ─────
            0
```

33. (A) 26.54 + 92.88 ≈ 27 + 93 = **120**
(C) 84.05 − 77.13 ≈ 84 − 77 = **7**
(D) 5.4 × 8 ≈ 5 × 8 = **40**
(E) 11.99 ÷ 3 ≈ 12 ÷ 3 = **4**
(I) 125.09 + 68.01 ≈ 125 + 68 = **193**
(L) 524.87 − 128.39 ≈ 525 − 128 = **397**
(M) 44.19 × 5 ≈ 44 × 5 = **220**
(S) 35.59 ÷ 6 ≈ 36 ÷ 6 = **6**

DECIMALS

34.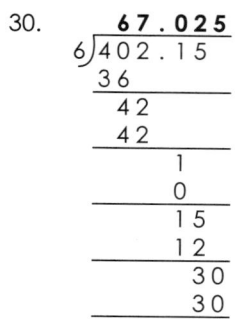

2.4 + 1.35 = 3.75 lb.
2.4 + 3.75 = 6.15 lb.
They bought **6.15 lb.** of meat altogether.

```
   2.40
 + 1.35
 ──────
   3.75

    1
   2.40
 + 3.75
 ──────
   6.15
```

35.
$43.05 + $12.20 = $55.25
$108.25 − $55.25 = $53
She had **$53** left.

```
   43.05
 + 12.20
 ──────
   55.25

   0 10
   1̶0̶8.25
 −  55.25
 ──────
   53.00
```

36. R: Rice S: Sugar
6 − 4.5 = 1.5 kg
Each bag of sugar has a mass of 1.5 kg.
5 × 1.5 = 7.5 kg
The mass of five bags of sugar is **7.5 kg**.

```
   5 10
   6̶.0̶
 − 4.5
 ─────
   1.5

    2
   1.5
 ×   5
 ─────
   7.5
```

37.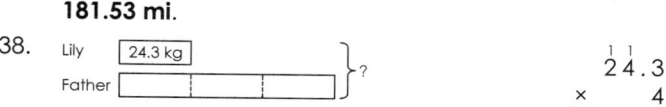

180.63 + 2.1 = 182.73 mi.
182.73 − 1.2 = 181.53 mi.
The distance the train traveled on Wednesday was **181.53 mi**.

```
   180.63
 +   2.1
 ───────
   182.73

   182.73
 −   1.2
 ───────
   181.53
```

38.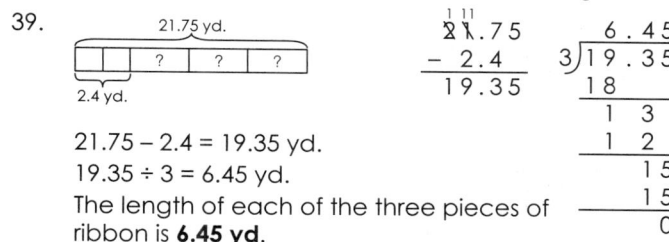

4 × 24.3 = 97.2 kg
The total mass of Lily and her father is **97.2 kg**.

```
    1 1
   24.3
 ×    4
 ──────
   97.2
```

39.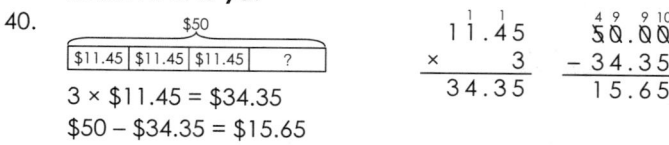

21.75 − 2.4 = 19.35 yd.
19.35 ÷ 3 = 6.45 yd.
The length of each of the three pieces of ribbon is **6.45 yd**.

```
    1 11
   2̶1̶.75
 −  2.4
 ──────
   19.35

      6.45
   3)19.35
      18
      ──
       1 3
       1 2
       ──
         15
         15
         ──
          0
```

40.
3 × $11.45 = $34.35
$50 − $34.35 = $15.65
He would receive **$15.65** in change.

```
    1 1
   11.45
 ×    3
 ──────
   34.35

   4 9 9 10
   5̶0̶.0̶0̶
 − 34.35
 ──────
   15.65
```

41. (a)
3 × 12.76 = 38.28 gal.
He would need **38.28 gal.** of paint if he wanted to paint three similar rooms.

```
    2 1
   12.76
 ×    3
 ──────
   38.28
```

(b) 38.28 × $5 = $191.40
Mr. Mendoza paid **$191.40** for the paint.

```
    4 1 4
   38.28
 ×     5
 ──────
  191.40
```

42.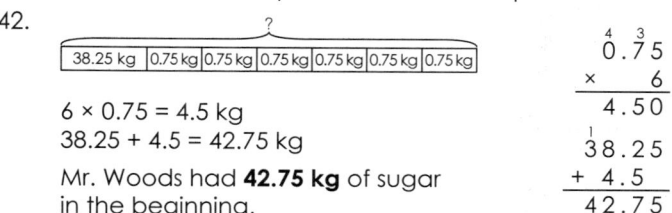

6 × 0.75 = 4.5 kg
38.25 + 4.5 = 42.75 kg
Mr. Woods had **42.75 kg** of sugar in the beginning.

```
    4 3
   0.75
 ×    6
 ──────
   4.50

   38.25
 +  4.5
 ──────
   42.75
```

43.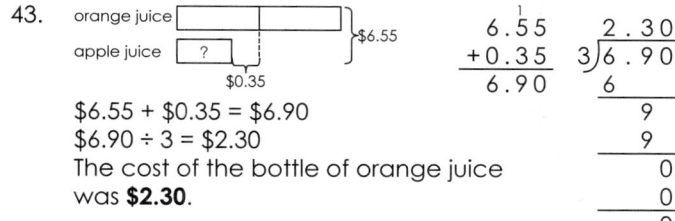

$6.55 + $0.35 = $6.90
$6.90 ÷ 3 = $2.30
The cost of the bottle of orange juice was **$2.30**.

```
    1
   6.55
 + 0.35
 ──────
   6.90

      2.30
   3)6.90
     6
     ──
      9
      9
      ──
       0
       0
       ──
        0
```

Review 1

1. **(3)**
The digit 8 is in the hundredths place.

2. **(2)**
$\frac{2 \times 2}{5 \times 2} = \frac{4}{10} = 0.4$

Singapore Math Practice Level 4B

3. **(3)**
 5.98 + 1.93 = 7.91
4. **(3)**
 $62.458 = 62\frac{458}{1,000}$ = 62 ones 458 thousandths
 = 62,458 thousandths
5. **(3)**
 37.46 ≈ 37.5
6. **(2)**
 ```
   3 2.0 7
 9)2 8 8.6 3
   2 7
   ---
     1 8
     1 8
     ---
         6
         0
         ---
         6 3
         6 3
         ---
           0
 ```
7. **(3)**
 12.99 + 5.5 ≈ 13 + 6 = 19
8. **540.701**
9. $1.68 = 1 + \frac{68}{100} = 1\frac{68}{100} = 1\frac{17}{25}$
10. **0.4**
11. **0.35**
 $9\frac{35}{100} = 9 + 0.35$
12. **5.2 gallons of water**
 1.9 + 2.1 + 1.2 = 5.2 gal.
13. **15.4**
 1.92 × 8 = 15.36
 15.36 ≈ 15.4
14. **19**
 305.419 = 3 hundreds 5 ones 4 tenths 1 hundredth
                 9 thousandths
 1 hundredth 9 thousandths = 19 thousandths
15. **5.6, 5.06, 5.006, 0.56**
16. **2.52 m**

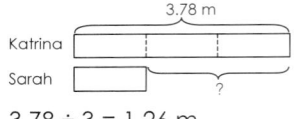

 3.78 ÷ 3 = 1.26 m
 2 × 1.26 = 2.52 m
17. **0.69 lb.**

 2.76 ÷ 4 = 0.69 lb.
18.

 2 × 12.9 = 25.8 mi.
 She travels a total of 25.8 mi. every day.

 5 × 25.8 = 129 mi.
 The total distance traveled by Elsie from Monday to Friday is **129 mi**.

19.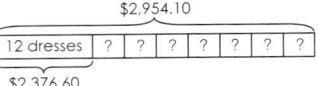

 $2,954.10 − $2,376.60 = $577.50
 $577.50 ÷ 7 = $82.50
 Each blouse cost **$82.50**.
20.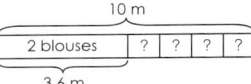

 10 − 3.6 = 6.4 m
 6.4 ÷ 4 = 1.6 m
 Sheila used **1.6 m** of cloth to sew each skirt.

Unit 11: Time

1. **30**
 When the second hand moves from 12 to 6, it is 30 sec.
2. **40**
 When the second hand moves from 3 to 11, it is 40 sec.
3. **35**
 When the second hand moves from 12 to 7, it is 35 sec.
4. **15**
 When the second hand moves from 9 to 12, it is 15 sec.
5. **30**
 When the second hand moves from 5 to 11, it is 30 sec.
6.
7.
8.
9.
10.
11. **6:38:06 P.M.**
12. **1:22:21 P.M.**
13. **4:40:35 A.M.**
14. **2:30:56 P.M.**
15. **1:02:18 P.M.**
16. **4:44:24 A.M.**

17. **11:06:05 A.M.**
18. **9:08:15 P.M.**
19. **4:51:05 P.M.**
20. **10:29:02 P.M.**
21. **30 min.**

    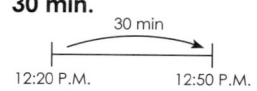
    12:20 P.M.   12:50 P.M.

22. **1 hr. 15 min.**

    30 min.   45 min.
    7:30 P.M.   8:00 P.M.   8:45 P.M.

    30 + 45 = 75 min = 1 hr. 15 min.

23. **8:45 A.M.**

    30 min.   15 min.
    8:00 A.M.   8:30 A.M. 8:45 A.M.

24. **2:40 P.M.**

    1 hr.   30 min.
    1:10 P.M.   2:10 P.M.   2:40 P.M.

35. **1:30 P.M.**

    1 hr.   1 hr.
    1:30 P.M.   2:30 P.M.   3:30 P.M.

26. **7:20 P.M.**

    45 min.   1 hr.   1 hr.   1 hr.
    7:20 P.M. 8:05 P.M. 9:05 P.M. 10:05 P.M. 11:05 P.M.

27.
    45 min.   2 hr.   30 min.
    5:15 P.M. 6 P.M.   8 P.M. 8:30 P.M.

    2 hr. + 45 min. + 30 min. = 2 hr. 75 min.
                                    = 3 hr. 15 min.
    He took **3 hr. 15 min.** to do his project.

28.
    10 min.   20 min.
    2:50 P.M. 3:00 P.M.   3:20 P.M.

    The correct time should be **2:50 P.M.**

29.
    25 min.
    1:15 P.M.   1:40 P.M.

    Benjamin left his house at **1:15 P.M.**

30.
    1 hr.   45 min.
    4:00 P.M. 5:00 P.M. 5:45 P.M.

    She spent **1 hr. 45 min.** at the shopping center.

31.
    3 hr.   15 min.
    8:40 P.M.   11:40 P.M. 11:55 P.M.

    The concert started at **8:40 P.M.**

32.
    1 hr.   30 min.
    12:40 P.M. 1:40 P.M. 2:10 P.M.

    The plane will reach Washington, D.C. at **2:10 P.M.**

33.
    2 hr.   30 min.
    8:05 A.M.   10:05 A.M. 10:35 A.M.

    The exam ended at **10:35 A.M.**

34.
    25 min.   8 hr.   15 min.
    10:35 P.M. 11 P.M.   7 A.M. 7:15 A.M.

    8 hr. + 25 min. + 15 min. = 8 hr. 40 min.
    The journey was **8 hr. 40 min.**

35.
    New York time   9:30 P.M. 10:00 P.M.   12:00 A.M. 1:00 A.M.
    San Francisco time 12:30 P.M. 1:00 P.M.   3:00 P.M. 4:00 P.M.

    The time in New York is **1 A.M.**

Unit 12: Perimeter and Area

1. **8**, **4**, **8**, **4**, **24**
   8, **4**, **32**
2. **7**, **7**, **7**, **7**, **28**
   7, **7**, **49**
3. **10**, **10**, **10**, **10**, **40**
   10, **10**, **100**
4. **9**, **18**, **9**, **18**, **54**
   9, **18**, **162**
5. **15**, **8**, **15**, **8**, **46**
   5, **5**, **25**
6. **17 in.**
   Perimeter = L + B + L + B
         44 = L + 5 + L + 5
         44 = L + L + 10
       44 − 10 = 2L
        34 ÷ 2 = L
            L = 17 in.
7. **13 cm**
   Length = 52 ÷ 4
          = 13 cm
8. **9 cm**
   Area = L × B
     36 = L × 4
       L = 36 ÷ 4
         = 9 cm
9. **11 yd.**
   Perimeter = 15 + B + 15 + B
        52 = 30 + B + B
    52 − 30 = 2B
     22 ÷ 2 = B
           B = 11 yd.
10. **9 ft.**
    Area = 81 ft.^{2}
        = 9 ft. × 9 ft.
       L = 9 ft.
11. **32 cm**
    Area = 64 cm^2
        = 8 cm × 8 cm
       L = 8 cm
    Perimeter = 4 × L
            = 4 × 8
            = 32 cm
12. **128 in.^{2}**
    L = 2B
    L + B + L + B = 2B + B + 2B + B
                       = 6B
    6B = 48 in.

121

Singapore Math Practice Level 4B

B = 48 ÷ 6 = 8 in.
L = 2 × B = 16 in.
Area = 8 × 16 = 128 in.²

13. **2 ft.²**
Perimeter = L + L + B + B
6 = L + L + 1 + 1
L + L = 6 − 2 = 4 ft.
L = 4 ÷ 2 = 2 ft.
Area = 2 × 1 = 2 ft.²

14. **16 m**
Area = L × L
16 m² = 4 m × 4 m
L = 4 m
Perimeter = 4 × 4 = 16 m

15. **50 yd.**
A = L × B
150 = $\frac{3}{2}$B × B
150 ÷ $\frac{3}{2}$ = B × B
150 × $\frac{2}{3}$ = B × B
100 = B × B
B = 10 yd.
L = $\frac{3}{2}$ × 10 = 15 yd.
Perimeter = 10 + 15 + 10 + 15
= 50 yd.

16. **46 cm**

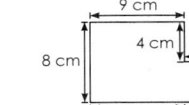

Perimeter
= 9 + 4 + 6 + 4 + 6 + 9 + 8
= 46 cm

17. **84 in.²**
Area of A = 16 × 3 = 48 in.²
Area of B = 9 × 3 = 27 in.²
Area of C = 3 × 3 = 9 in.²
Total area = 48 + 27 + 9 = 84 in.²

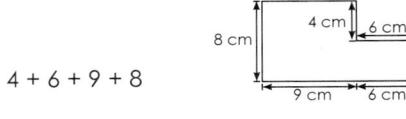

18.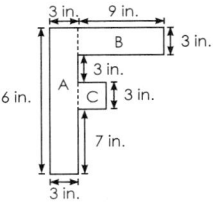
Area of A = 7 × 1 = 7 cm²
Area of B = 10 × 4 = 40 cm²
Area of C = 14 × 5 = 70 cm²
Total area = 7 + 40 + 70 = **117 cm²**
Perimeter = 7 + 1 + 1 + 4 + 2 + 5 + 14 + 10 = **44 cm**

19.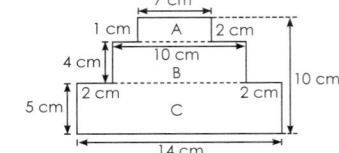

Area of A = 18 × 8 = 144 m²
Area of B = 9 × 12 = 108 m²
Area of C = 15 × 8 = 120 m²
Total area = 144 + 108 + 120 = **372 m²**
Perimeter = 8 + 3 + 17 + 15 + 8 + 3 + 9 + 3 + 8 + 18
= **92 m**

20.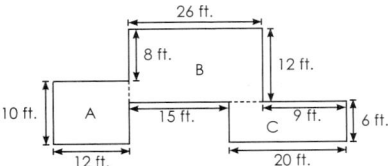

Area of A = 10 × 12 = 120 ft.²
Area of B = 26 × 12 = 312 ft.²
Area of C = 20 × 6 = 120 ft.²
Total area = 120 + 312 + 120 = **552 ft.²**.
Perimeter
= 26 + 12 + 9 + 6 + 20 + 6 + 15 + 6 + 12 + 10 + 12 + 8
= **142 ft.**

21.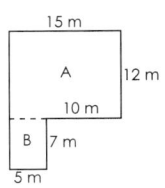
Area of A = 15 × 12 = 180 m²
Area of B = 7 × 5 = 35 m²
180 + 35 = 215 m²
Her house is **215 m²**.

22. Area of exhibition hall = 16 × 15 = 240 ft.².
Area that is not covered with carpet
= 9 × 8
= 72 ft.²
240 − 72 = 168 ft.²
The area that is covered with carpet is **168 ft.²**.

23. Area of one square = 294 ÷ 6 = 49 cm² = 7 × 7
Length of each square = 7 cm
12 × 7 = 84 cm
The perimeter of the shaded portion is **84 cm**.

24. Area of the larger rectangular board
= L × B
= (28 + 3 + 3) × (16 + 3 + 3)
= 34 × 22
= 748 in.²
Area of the white rectangular board = L × B
= 28 × 16
= 448 in.²
748 − 448 = 300 in.²
The area not covered by the white rectangular board is **300 in.²**.

25. Area of Mary's room = L × B
= 8 × 7
= 56 m²
Area not covered by the carpet = L × B
= 4.5 × 4
= 18 m²
56 − 18 = 38 m²
The floor area in her room that is covered by carpet is **38 m²**.

26. (a) (15 + 2 + 2) + (11 + 2 + 2) = 34 yd.
       2 × 34 = 68 yd.
       The length of the fence was **68 yd.**
   (b) 68 × $3.85 = $261.80
       It cost **$261.80** to put a fence round the plot of land.
27. Area of the square cardboard = L × L
                                 = 35 × 35
                                 = 1,225 cm²
    Area of the "L" shape = (19 × 5) + (25 × 6)
                          = 245 cm²
    1,225 − 245 = 980 cm²
    The remaining area of the cardboard was **980 cm².**

Review 2

1. **(2)**
   Width = 32 ÷ 2 = 16 in.
   Perimeter = 32 + 16 + 32 + 16 = 96 in.
2. **(2)**
3. **(4)**
   Perimeter = 4 × 256 = 1,024 m
   6 × 1,024 = 6,144 m
4. **(2)**
   When the second hand moves from 2 to 6, it is 20 sec.
5. **(3)**
   6 + 6 + 3 + 3 + 3 + 6 + 6 + 15 = 48 ft.
6. **(1)**
   64 − 19 − 19 = 26 cm
   26 ÷ 2 = 13 cm
7. **(2)**
   1 hr. + 20 min. + 15 min. = 1 hr. 35 min.
8. Length = 40 ÷ 4 = 10 yd.
   Area = 10 × 10 = **100 yd.²**
9. **540 cm²**
   Area A = 8 × 11 = 88 cm²
   Area B = 16 × 11 = 176 cm²
   Area C = 30 × 8 = 240 cm²
   88 + 176 + 240 = 504 cm²

   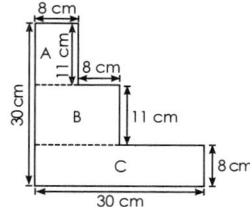

10. **8 ft.**
    Area of each square = 256 ÷ 4 = 64 ft.² = 8 × 8
    Length of each square = 8 ft.
11. **84 in.**
    Area of A = 12 × 12 = 144 in.²
           144 = L × 8
             L = 144 ÷ 8 = 18 in.
    Perimeter = 12 + 12 + 4 + 18 + 8 + 18 + 12 = 84 in.
12. **112 m²**
    Area of bigger rectangle = 20 × 14 = 280 m²
    Area of smaller rectangle = 14 × 12 = 168 m²
    Area of shaded part = 280 − 168 = 112 m²
13. **1:15 P.M.**
14. **10:22:43 P.M.**
15. (clock showing time)
16. (a) Area of swimming pool = 15 × 12 = 180 ft.²
       Area of swimming pool with 2-foot wide pavement
       = (15 + 2 + 2) × (12 + 2 + 2)
       = 19 × 16
       = 304 ft.²
       304 − 180 = 124 ft.²
       The area of pavement Mr. Edmonds needs to tile is **124 ft.².**
    (b) 124 × $29 = $3,596
        He has to pay **$3,596.**
17. 2 hr. + 7 hr. + 30 min. + 55 min. = 9 hr. 85 min.
                                      = 10 hr. 25 min.
    He works **10 hours 25 minutes** every night.
18. 49 cm² = 7 cm × 7 cm
    The length of square X is 7 cm.
    81 cm² = 9 cm × 9 cm
    The length of square Y is 9 cm
    7 + 9 + 7 + 7 + 7 + 2 + 9 + 2 + 7 + 7 = 64
    The perimeter of the figure is **64 cm.**
19. $\frac{3}{5}$ × 120 = 72 in.
    Its width is 72 in.
    120 × 72 = 8,640 in.²
    The area of the cardboard is **8,640 in.².**
20. She should make the call at **1:00 P.M.** in Denver.

Unit 13: Symmetry

1. Yes
2. Yes
3. Yes
4. Yes
5. Yes

6. No
7. No
8. Yes
9. No
10. Yes
11. No
12. Yes
13. No
14. No
15. Yes
16.
17.
18.
19.
20.
21.

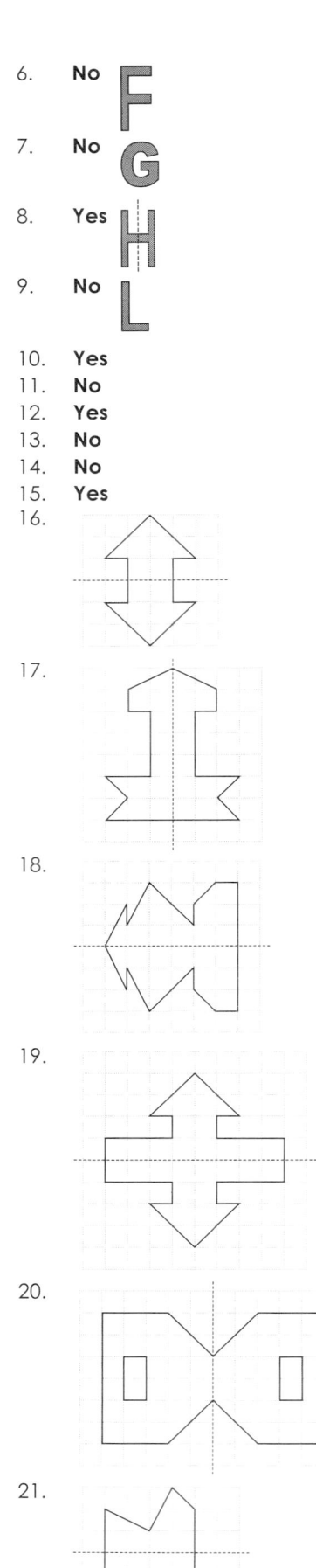

22.
23.
24.
25.
26.
27.

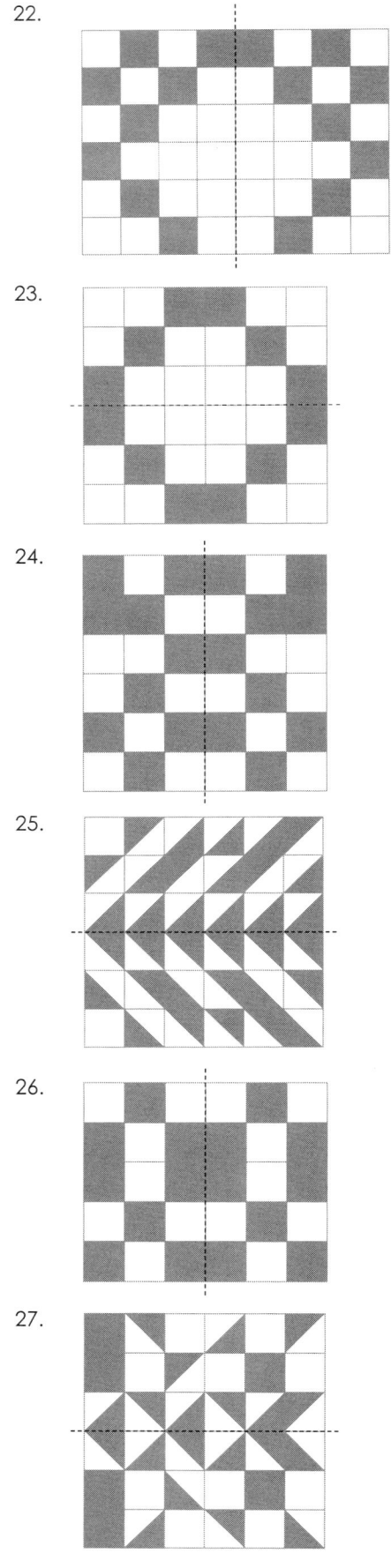

Unit 14: Tessellations

For questions 1 to 5, accept other correct answers.

1.
2.
3.
4.
5.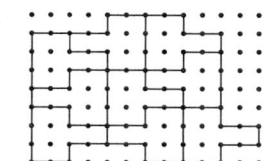
6. **No**
   The gaps show that the shape does not tessellate.
7. **Yes**
8. **No**
   The gaps show that the shape does not tessellate.
9. **Yes**
10. **Yes**
11.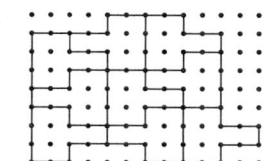
12.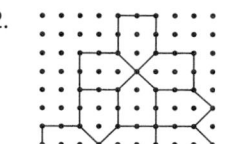
13.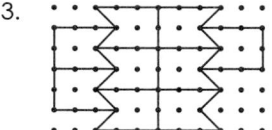
14.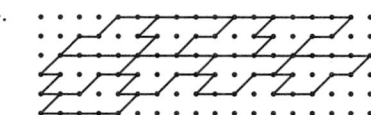
15.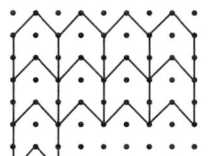
16. (a)
    (b)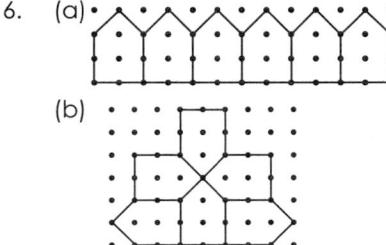
17. (a)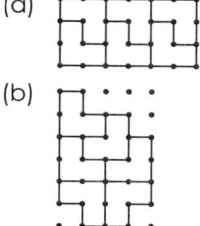
    (b)

Review 3

1. **(2)**
2. **(2)**
3. **(3)**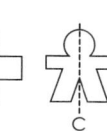
4. **(4)**
5. **(2)**
6. **(3)**
7. **(2)**
8. **Yes**
9.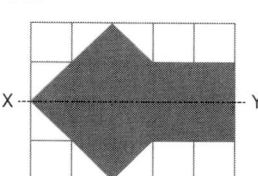
10.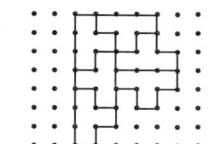
11. Accept other correct answers.
    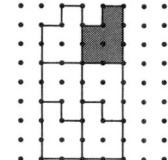
12. **Yes**
13.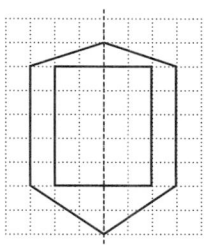
14.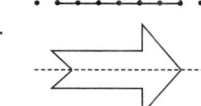
15.

Singapore Math Practice Level 4B

16. **No**
17. *Accept other correct answers.*

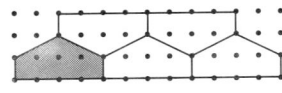

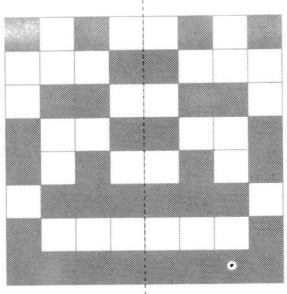

19. **No**
20.

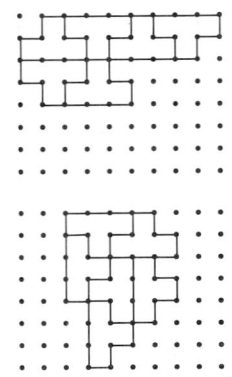

Final Review

1. **(3)**
   28.16 + 5.09 = 33.25
2. **(2)**
   4 m 60 cm ≈ 5 m
3. **(3)**
   When the second hand moves from 3 to 8, it is 25 sec.
4. **(1)**
5. **(4)**
   8.604 = 8 + 0.6 + 0.004
6. **(2)**
7. **(4)**
   40 + 1.5 + 0.03 = 41.53
8. **(3)**
9. **(1)**
   64 ÷ 4 = 16 in.
10. **(2)**
    405 hundredths = $\frac{405}{100} = 4\frac{5}{100} = 4.05$
11. **(4)**
    93.28 × 8 = 746.24
12. **(3)**
13. **(2)**

    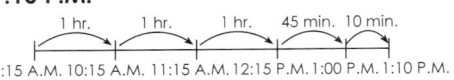

    1 hr. + 30 min. + 10 min. = 1 hr. 40 min.

14. **(2)**
    5.4 ÷ 4 = 1.35
15. **(1)**
    100 ÷ 10 = 10
    10 × $2.05 = $20.50
16. **(1)**
    18.35 − 3.2 = 15.15 sec.
17. **(2)**
    Length = 20 ÷ 4 = 5 ft.
    Area = 5 × 5 = 25 ft.²
18. **(3)**
    Perimeter = 12 × 4 = 48 cm
19. **(2)**
    9.9 ≈ 10
20. **(4)**
    The digit 9 is in the thousandths place.
21. **0.5**
    $\frac{8}{16} = \frac{1 \times 5}{2 \times 5} = \frac{5}{10} = 0.5$
22. **1:10 P.M.**

    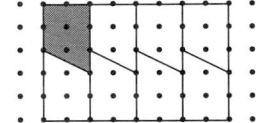

23. **0.8**
    $\frac{4 \times 2}{5 \times 2} = \frac{8}{10} = 0.8$
24. **Shade any 3 squares.**
    $\frac{25}{100} \times 12 = 3$
25. **Yes**

26. *Accept other correct answers.*

    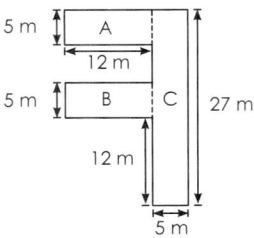

27. **7.8, 7.08, 0.78**
28. **255 m²**

    Area of A = 12 × 5 = 60 m²
    Area of B = 12 × 5 = 60 m²
    Area of C = 27 × 5 = 135 m²
    Total area = 60 + 60 + 135 = 255 m²

29.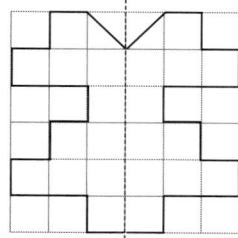

30. **7**
    $41.8 ÷ 6 ≈ 42 ÷ 6 = 7$

31. **5:25 P.M.**
    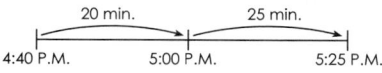

32. **180 ft.²**
    $18 ÷ 3 = 6$ ft.
    Area of 1 square = $6 × 6 = 36$ ft.²
    Area of 5 squares = $36 × 5 = 180$ ft.²

33.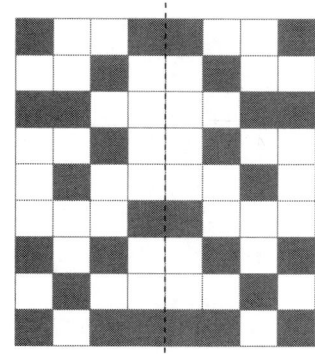

34. **1.8 gallons of syrup.**
    $9 ÷ 5 = 1.8$ gal.

35.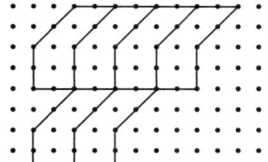

36. **44 yd.**
    Area = L × 6
    $96 = L × 6$
    $L = 96 ÷ 6 = 16$ yd.
    Perimeter = $16 + 6 + 16 + 6 = 44$ yd.

37. **tenths**

38. **15.02, 15.13**

39. **11:35 A.M.**
    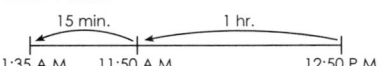

40. **No**

41. $13 × \$9.65 = \$125.45$

    $\$150 - \$125.45 = \$24.55$
    She received **$24.55** in change.

42.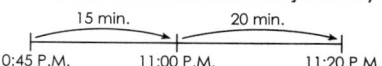
    The coach stopped for a rest at 10:45 P.M.

    The coach continued the journey at 11:20 P.M.

    $15 + 20 = 35$ min.
    It stopped **35 min.** for a rest.

43.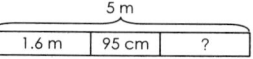
    $0.84 + 0.47 + 0.65 = 1.96$ L
    $12 × 1.96 = 23.52$ L
    There are **23.52 L** of fruit punch in a dozen bottles.

44.
    $0.95 + 1.6 = 2.55$ m   [95 cm = 0.95 m]
    $5 - 2.55 = 2.45$ m
    She had **2.45 m** of ribbon left.

45. $18 - 3 - 3 = 12$ yd.
    $12 × 12 = 144$ yd.
    $144 × \$19 = \$2,736$
    The total cost of the carpet is **$2,736**.

Challenge Questions

1.

2. **3 P.M.**

3. $2 × \$919.70 = \$1,839.40$
   Four television sets and two DVD players cost $1,839.40.
   $\$1,839.40 - \$639.70 = \$1,199.70$
   Three television sets cost **$1,199.70**.

4. Area of bigger square = 576 in.² = $24 × 24$
   Length of bigger square = 24 in.
   Area of shaded square = 144 in.² = $12 × 12$
   Length of shaded square = 12 in.
   $2x = 24 - 12 = 12$ in.
   $x = 12 ÷ 2 =$ **6 in.**

Singapore Math Practice Level 4B

5. Perimeter = (8 × 3) + (6 × 3) + (6 × 3) + (4 × 3)
   = **72 cm**

6.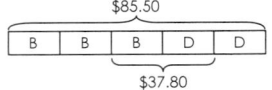

   2 L 600 mL ÷ 2 = 1 L 300 mL

   8 × 1 L 300 mL = 10 L 400 mL

   Mrs. Munoz sold **10 L 400 mL** of lemon tea over the weekend.

7. 3 × 3 × 3 = 27 in.³
   27 cubes are needed to make this 3-in. solid.

8.

   B: Book
   D: Dictionary

   $85.50 – $37.80 = $47.70

   Two books and a dictionary cost $47.70.

   $47.70 – $37.80 = $9.90

   Each book is **$9.90**.

9.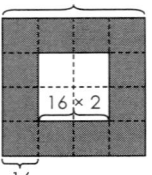

   64 ÷ 4 = 16 cm
   16 × 2 = 32 cm
   Area of the unshaded square = 32 × 32 = **1,024 cm²**

10. A Ⓢ V M Ⓚ

11. 5 × 5 × 5 = 125 cm³
    3,125 ÷ 125 = 25
    25 5-cm cubes are needed to form a solid of 3,125 cm³.

12. 1 hour → 5 chairs
    8 hours → 5 × 8 = 40 chairs
    120 ÷ 40 = 3
    He took **3 days** to paint 120 similar chairs.